Countdown
to Christmas

Countdown to Christmas

Edited by Mary Cadogan

with principal photography by Marie-Louise Avery

Contents

Recipes marked with this symbol are
designed to be given as gifts

Introduction

I have been preparing family Christmas feasts for over twenty-five years, but the magic never wears off. I absolutely love being in the country at this time of year– still, clear, frosty mornings, gathering holly and mistletoe from the hedgerows, fire blazing in the hearth– but I know all too well that the hectic preparations can very often leave the cook feeling exhausted. In this book I will be sharing with you my hints and tips for creating the perfect Christmas, and will show how a little time spent planning ahead will help ensure a much more enjoyable Christmas for the cook.

If you have never hosted Christmas before, this book will guide you through all the dishes you are likely to need, from the easiest Christmas cake you will ever make, to the essential recipes for Christmas lunch itself. Advice is given on everything from how to prepare and cook your turkey to making perfect gravy and preparing delicious vegetables that are cooked to perfection. To help ensure that everything reaches the table on time, we have included a detailed timeplan which will take you right through from turning on the oven to sitting down to a delicious lunch. To make life even easier, we have added an essential shopping list – at such a busy time it is so easy to forget a crucial ingredient.

Whatever entertaining you are planning to do over the festive season, this book will provide all the answers. I challenged *Good Food*'s favourite celebrity chefs to come up with some extra special Christmas recipes and the mouth-watering dishes they created are all included here. What could be more perfect for a cosy dinner party than Ainsley Harriott's Roast Pork with Chilli Mango Stuffing, followed by either Chocolate Chestnut Log, or a glamorous Mango and Almond Trifle? And if you are having vegetarian friends round for a festive meal, Gary Rhodes' Vegetarian Christmas Feast is the perfect solution.

For the more experienced cook, the recipes in this book provide plenty of inspiration. Recipes from top chefs include a stunning dinner party menu that freezes beautifully: Tony Tobin devised a deceptively simple Chicken and Clementine Tagine and to follow Paul Rankin created a fabulous Chocolate Mousse Cake – a definite challenge, but worth every minute of your time.

To help you plan your time more easily we have started our countdown twelve weeks before Christmas and suggested what you may like to make each week. Of course everybody's schedule is different, what you see here is just a framework that you can easily adapt to your own needs. If you find, for example, that you haven't made the Christmas pudding eleven weeks in advance, don't worry, you can make it on Christmas Eve if that suits you better; it will still taste wonderful. Many of the recipes include information on preparing ahead and freezing, so you can work out your own timetable if you prefer. Making Christmas easier and more enjoyable is the purpose of the countdown, not to load you with guilt if you haven't managed to cook everything you had planned. Use it in the way you find most helpful and if you run out of time, cheat like mad.

Of course making your own of everything is a fantastic goal, but I hope this book will give you the confidence to plan your Christmas in a way that suits you best. If you prefer to buy your cranberry sauce and brandy butter, but would willingly spend hours decorating the cake, that's your choice and if it works for you, that's great. I am sure you will find, though, that making as many things as you can in advance means you are not left trying to do everything at the last minute. Make sure you get the rest of the family to lend a hand so that Christmas can be a pleasure for all, especially the cook.

Scattered throughout the book are gift ideas for food-loving friends. I particularly enjoy making edible gifts and spending time wrapping them beautifully, especially when I know they will be greatly appreciated and enjoyed by the recipient. Something that you have made yourself and spent precious time and effort on will always give special pleasure. Save or buy beautiful jars to show off Cranberry and Clementine Marmalade or to fill with Phil Vickery's Red Onion and Apricot Chutney, and pour Rosemary and Lemon Oil into elegant bottles with hand written labels. Home-made Chocolate truffles are a perfect gift if you are visiting friends for a meal and our Christmas pudding also makes a lovely present, particularly if you make a round one. Wrap in the usual way, then overwrap in cellophane and tie with a wide gold or silver ribbon. Don't forget to attach a label giving re-heating and storage instructions.

Finally, if you're on a special diet, or cooking for someone who is, there's no need to go without those seasonal classics: the mince pies and the Christmas Pudding. We have included some gluten-free recipes that are full of festive flavour.

I hope that, by using this book, the run-up to Christmas will be a more pleasurable experience for everyone and, most of all, I hope that it will help you enjoy the best Christmas ever.

Best wishes for a very happy Christmas.

Mary Cadee

Countdown Calendar

If you're following our countdown, by the time November arrives you will already have made your Christmas cake, pudding and mince pies. There are still, however, a lot of jobs to be done, so to guide you through the final hectic weeks, use this calendar as a basis for your preparations.

NOVEMBER

1	Go through the cupboards to make way for all the Christmas food.	16	
2	Do the same with the freezer. Plan a couple of meals to use up the things you discover.	17	
3	Make and freeze Lesley Waters' Freeze-ahead Spicy Cigars (page 22).	18	Make and freeze the dough for the Stilton and Walnut Crunchies (page 28).
4		19	
5	Check you have enough plates and glasses.	20	
6		21	
7	Make a shopping list of things to buy now such as food basics, matches, candles, paper napkins and kitchen foil.	22	
8	Make and freeze the Chocolate Chestnut Log on page 26.	23	Make the first part of the Freeze-ahead Dinner Party – Tony Tobin's Chicken and Clementine Tagine (page 34).
9		24	
10	If you want a boozy Christmas cake, remember to keep feeding it weekly with brandy.	25	Buy the Christmas Crackers while there is still some choice.
11		26	
12	Decide what drinks you will need over the festive season and make a list of things to buy.	27	Make Paul Rankin's Chocolate Mousse Cake to round off the freeze-ahead menu (page 38).
13		28	Shop for wines, spirits and mixers. Arrange delivery if possible.
14	Order the turkey. Turn to page 92 to decide on the right size.	29	
15	Make Phil Vickery's delicious Red Onion and Apricot Chutney (page 30).	30	

DECEMBER

1	
2	
3	Cook Glazed Ham with Caramelized Fruits (page 42) for supper with friends. Leftovers are perfect for a cold lunch.
4	
5	Update your shopping lists. Plan what is still needed for everyday cooking, entertaining and Christmas food.
6	If you're entertaining vegetarians, make and freeze Gary Rhodes's Vegetarian Christmas Feast (page 46).
7	
8	Order extras from the milkman such as cream, juice and mineral water. (Less to carry home.)
9	
10	Make the marzipan stars for the cake and leave to dry (Starry Christmas Cake, page 52). Invite friends round and serve-up your Freeze-ahead Dinner Party menu.
11	
12	Decorate the Christmas cake.
13	Make and freeze the Cranberry Sauce (page 51). Freeze the breadcrumbs for the bread sauce.
14	
15	Make the Brandy Butter (page 50) to serve with the Light and Crumbly Christmas Pudding (page 12).
16	
17	
18	If you're having a drinks party, prepare the canapés (page 60).
19	Cook the Stilton and Walnut Crunchies (dough already made and frozen). Make the Pistachio Chocolate Brittle (page 54) and the Super-rich Chocolate Truffles (page 55).
20	
21	Make the Festive Almond Biscuits (page 68). Wrap-up all the edible gifts ready to give as presents.
22	Defrost your Festive Mince Pies (page 20) ready for any visitors.
23	Shop early for all the last-minute fresh food. Make Ainsley's Roast Pork with Chilli Mango Stuffing for a special dinner (page 70). Serve the Chocolate Chestnut Log (already made and frozen) for pudding.
24	Collect the turkey. Stuff the red onions (page 86) . Make the Sausagemeat and Thyme Koftas (page 88). Prepare the Mango and Almond Trifle (page 74) as an alternative to Christmas pudding. Make the Lemon and Lime Butter for the turkey (page 84).
25	Follow the timeplan (page 83) for your perfect Christmas lunch.

Moist  and Fruity
Christmas Cake

This cake keeps for up to three months – made now, it will be in perfect shape by Christmas. Fabulously moist and buttery, it's packed with all the wonderful Christmassy fruits and spices – not to mention the alcohol. (If you want a non-alcoholic cake, replace the brandy or sherry with the same amount of orange or apple juice.) The mixture is made in a saucepan, which saves on washing-up.

Preparation: 1¹⁄₂ hours
Cooking: 3–3¹⁄₂ hours
Makes: a 20 cm/8 in round or 18 cm/7 in square cake

225 g/8 oz butter, chopped, plus extra for greasing
300 g/10 oz dark muscovado sugar
2 × 500 g bags luxury mixed dried fruit
finely grated rind and juice of 1 orange
finely grated rind and juice of 1 lemon
125 ml/4 fl oz brandy or sherry
100 g packet whole blanched almonds
4 large eggs, lightly beaten
100 g packet ground almonds
300 g/10 oz plain flour
¹⁄₂ teaspoon baking powder
1 teaspoon mixed spice
1 teaspoon ground cinnamon
¹⁄₂ teaspoon freshly grated nutmeg

One Put the butter, sugar, dried fruit, citrus rinds and juices, and brandy or sherry in a large pan and bring slowly to the boil, stirring until the butter has melted, then reduce the heat and let it bubble gently for 10 minutes, stirring occasionally (picture 1). Meanwhile cut a double-thickness strip of greaseproof paper 5 cm/ 2 in deeper than your cake tin and long enough to wrap around the tin with a slight overlap. Make a 2.5 cm/1 in crease along the long folded edge, then snip the paper up to the crease at regular intervals. Cut 2 rounds or squares of paper to fit the base of the tin (draw around the tin with a pencil on to double-thickness paper, then cut along the pencil line). Grease the tin, then line the base with one piece of paper. Grease the paper then fit the long strip of paper around the sides with the snipped edge flat on the base of the tin. Grease the paper and fit the second piece of paper over the top. Preheat the oven to 150°C/Gas 2; fan oven: cook from cold at 130°C.

Two Remove the pan from the heat and leave to cool for about 30 minutes. Toast the whole almonds in a dry frying pan, tossing them until they are evenly browned (this helps to bring out the flavour). When cool enough to handle, chop them roughly. Stir the eggs, and the chopped and ground almonds, into the cooled fruit mixture and mix well. Set a sieve over the pan and sift the flour, baking powder and spices into the pan (picture 2). Stir in gently but thoroughly until there are no traces of flour left.

Three Spoon the mixture into the tin and spread it out evenly (picture 3).

Four Dip a large metal spoon into boiling water, then smooth over the cake mixture to level. Bake for 1 hour, then reduce the heat to 140°C/Gas 1/fan oven 120°C and bake for a further 2–2½ hours until the cake is dark golden and firm to touch. Cover the top with foil if it starts to darken too much.

Five To see if the cake is ready, insert a fine skewer into the centre – if it comes out clean the cake is cooked (picture 4). If it is not cooked, return to the oven for 15 minutes, then test again. Repeat until the cake is cooked. Allow the cake to cool in the tin for 15 minutes, then turn out, peel off the paper and cool on a wire rack. Wrap in double-thickness greaseproof paper, then overwrap in foil.

✱ FEEDING THE CAKE: For a more boozy cake, feed it with extra brandy after baking. Invert the cake and make holes all over the base with a fine skewer. Spoon 2 tablespoons of brandy over the holes until it soaks in. Rewrap cake and repeat weekly until ready to ice (see my Starry Cake on page 52).

✱ STORING THE CAKE: Store the cake, well wrapped in double-thickness greaseproof paper and overwrapped in foil, in a cool dry place – damp warm conditions could turn it mouldy. Any leftover cake can be frozen up to a year if un-iced, or up to 3 months if iced.

Light and Crumbly
Christmas Pudding

This Christmas pudding is just the way I like it – moist, crumbly, not at all dark or heavy – and made with butter instead of suet to give it a better flavour. And you can choose whichever fruits you like – not just the familiar ones. As a bonus, the pudding is steamed in the oven: you don't have to top up the water so often and the kitchen windows don't get fogged up. You can eat one pudding this year and save the other for next year; but if you want to make just one, then the ingredients are easily halved.

800 g/1 lb 12 oz mixed dried fruit
   of your choice, e.g. dates, figs,
   apricots, glacé cherries,
   currants, raisins, cranberries
   or pineapple

grated rind and juice of 1 lemon

grated rind and juice of 1 orange

125 ml/4 fl oz brandy or sherry

225 g/8 oz softened butter, plus
   extra for greasing

225 g/8 oz dark muscovado sugar

4 eggs, lightly beaten

50 g/2 oz blanched almonds,
   toasted and chopped

100 g/4 oz self-raising flour

1 teaspoon each of mixed spice,
   nutmeg, ginger and cinnamon

100 g/4 oz fresh white breadcrumbs

Preparation: 30 minutes, plus up to 4
days soaking

Cooking: 3–4 hours

Makes: two 1.2 litre/2 pint puddings,
each enough for 8

14

One If any of the dried fruits you are using are too large, chop them into smaller pieces (picture 1).

Two Put the mixed fruit, citrus rinds and juices, and brandy or sherry in a large bowl, stir and cover with a tea towel; leave for 2–4 days, stirring occasionally (picture 2).

Three Preheat the oven to 160°C/Gas 3; fan oven: cook from cold at 140°C. Butter two 1.2 litre/ 2 pint pudding basins and line the bases with a circle of greaseproof paper. Beat together the butter and sugar until the mixture is pale and fluffy; this should take about 5 minutes in a food processor, or 10 minutes by hand. Transfer to a large bowl. Gradually beat in the eggs, beating well after each addition – don't worry if the mixture curdles as it won't affect the taste.

Tip in the fruit, soaking liquid and almonds, and stir well. Get the family to help and everyone make a wish. Sift flour and spices, add breadcrumbs, and fold in well.

Four Fill the pudding basins with the mixture to within 2.5 cm/1 in of the top. Cover each with double-thickness greaseproof paper, pleated in the centre; tie down with string. Do this by wrapping a doubled length of kitchen string around the top rim of the basin. Thread one end through the loop and tie with a double knot, pulling it tightly to lock in place. Overtie to secure in place (pictures 3, 4). Trim off the excess paper, then overwrap with foil, tucking it under the greaseproof. Put the basin in a large roasting tin and pour in about 5 cm/2 in of boiling water (picture 5).

Five Cover the tin with a double-thickness tent of foil, sealing the edges tightly (picture 6). Bake for 3–4 hours until the puddings have risen, are firm to the touch and darker. You may have to top up with water.

✻ PREPARING AHEAD: This pudding can be made up to a year before you eat it. After the initial steaming, remove the foil and paper and replace with fresh. Store in a cool dry place, labelling it with the date you made it. Every couple of months feed with a tablespoon or two of brandy or sherry (see the tip on page 11). Reheat as above.

✻ TOASTING NUTS: Cook almonds in a dry frying pan over a low heat for 5 minutes, swirling the pan now and then so they brown evenly.

✽ TO REHEAT THE PUDDING:
Replace the paper and foil. Lower
one pudding into a large pan; pour
in boiling water to come a third of
the way up the basin. Cover tightly
and steam for 2 hours. Or reheat
in the microwave: remove the foil
and microwave in a 750W oven on
Medium for 6–8 minutes; leave to
rest for 2 minutes.

✽ TO MAKE A ROUND
PUDDING: Use half the recipe to
fill a 900 g/2 lb mould and the
full quantity for a 1.8 kg/4 lb
mould. Liberally butter both
halves of the mould. Put the
mixture in one half of the mould
and pile it up in the centre. Cover
with the other half and lock into
place. Steam as above.

✽ HIDING CHARMS: If you're
hiding charms in the pudding,
add them just before reheating.
Sterilize them or wrap in foil first.

Cranberry and Clementine
Marmalade

This softly set marmalade will ensure you are thought about every breakfast time. It keeps unopened for up to 4 months, so you'll have plenty of time to plan when to make it; once opened, it should be used within a month.

600 g/1 lb 5 oz clementines

4 lemons

225 g/8 oz fresh or frozen cranberries

1.6 kg/3½ lb preserving or granulating sugar

150 ml/¼ pint whisky

Preparation: 25 minutes
Cooking: 1¼–1½ hours
Makes: about 2.2 kg/5 lb

One Halve the clementines and lemons and squeeze the juice (reserve the pips). Tie the pips and lemon halves in a piece of muslin. Thinly or thickly slice the clementine rind, removing any pith; put in a preserving pan. Add the squeezed juice, the muslin bag and 1.2 litres/2 pints water.

Two Bring to the boil, then simmer gently for 1 hour or until the peel is tender. Remove the muslin bag, squeezing out the juice.

Three Add the cranberries and cook for 2 minutes until they start to break up. Add the sugar, stirring until dissolved. Stir in the whisky.

Bring to the boil and boil rapidly for 20–35 minutes until setting point is reached. (Spoon a little of the liquid on to a saucer and chill for a few minutes. The mixture should wrinkle when pushed with your finger.) Leave the mixture to stand for 15 minutes. Ladle into sterilized jars. Seal well.

✱ HOW TO WRAP IN STYLE: Stand each glass jar inside a square cardboard box and stuff the spaces with scraps of tissue paper to protect the jars. Wrap the box in a large square of muslin, tied in place with wide gingham ribbon. Tie on a small spoon as a clue to the contents.

Rosemary and Lemon Oil

Flavoured oils are so versatile and make great gifts. They can be used in marinades and salad dressings, or splashed over bruschetta, roasted vegetables and fish. Choose small glass bottles with tight-fitting caps, as flavoured oil doesn't keep as long as unflavoured.

long sprigs of fresh rosemary

lemons

dry or brined pink
peppercorns

olive oil

Wash and dry the rosemary sprigs and lemons. Push several rosemary sprigs down to the base of each bottle. Pare several strips of lemon rind and push them down into the bottle too. Dry the peppercorns on kitchen paper if using brined, then scatter a teaspoonful into each bottle. Pour in the olive oil, filling up to the rim, and replace the stopper.

Before giving as presents, allow 1–2 weeks for the flavours to blend.

✱ HOW TO WRAP IN STYLE:
A simple wrapping is all you need to disguise the bottle. Cut a length of baking parchment or Japanese hand-made paper the same width as your bottle is high, and long enough to wrap around it twice. Wrap it round the bottle, securing with a piece of sticky tape. Cut a length of wide dark green or brown organza ribbon (enough to go twice around the bottle). Tie in place with green garden string and tuck in a few sprigs of rosemary.

Preparation: 5 minutes

Cranberry and Orange Mincemeat

This melt-in-the mouth mincemeat is fruitier and less sweet than traditional mincemeat – there's no suet in it, which lightens the texture too. It's perfect made now for Christmas, kept in a cool, dark place. Or, of course, you could use it now if you decide to make and freeze your own mince pies ahead of time – see the following recipe for Festive Mince Pies.

1 kg/2 lb 4 oz cooking apples

1 teaspoon mixed spice

1 teaspoon ground cinnamon

200 g/8 oz dark muscovado sugar

grated rind and juice of 3 oranges

grated rind and juice of 1 lemon

350 g/12 oz mixed dried fruit

100 g/4 oz dried apricots, chopped

350 g/12 oz cranberries, fresh or frozen

175 g/6 oz toasted flaked almonds

300 ml/½ pint brandy, rum or sherry

✱ TO KEEP LONGER: This mincemeat is not meant to be kept indefinitely – if you want to store it for more than 4 weeks pack it in small boxes in the freezer for up to 6 months.

✱ WHY COOKING APPLES? Cooking apples such as Bramleys cook to a smooth fluffy pulp, while eating apples tend to keep their shape. The apple pulp makes a smooth flavoursome base for the dried fruits, nuts and spices and means there is no need to add suet to keep the mincemeat moist.

One Peel, core and chop the apples, then put in a large pan with the spices, sugar, citrus rinds and juices. Bring to the boil, then cover and simmer for about 10 minutes until the apples start to soften. Add the dried fruit, apricots, cranberries, almonds and brandy, rum or sherry. Bring to the boil, stirring well, then reduce the heat and simmer for 10 minutes.

Two Remove from the heat, leave to cool, then pack the mincemeat into warm, sterilized jars, seal, label and keep for up to 4 weeks in a cool dry place.

Preparation: 30 minutes

Cooking: 20 minutes

Makes: about 1.8 kg/4 lb

Festive Mince Pies

Here are some mince pies with a difference, using my Cranberry and Orange Mincemeat.

FOR THE PASTRY

200 g/8 oz plain flour

50 g/2 oz ground almonds

140 g/5 oz butter, chopped
   into small pieces

grated rind of 1 orange

50 g/2 oz caster sugar

1 egg yolk

FOR THE FILLING AND DECORATION

200 g/8 oz mincemeat

1 egg white, lightly whisked

caster sugar, for dusting

One Preheat the oven to
200°C/Gas 6/fan oven 190°C.
Put the flour, almonds, butter,
orange rind and sugar into a food
processor and whizz into crumbs.
Add the egg yolk and a teaspoon
of cold water and pulse until it
forms a dough. Wrap in plastic film
and chill for 30 minutes.

Two Roll out the dough thinly and
stamp out 18 × 7.5 cm/3 in rounds
(picture 1). Use to line one and a
half 12-hole bun tins.

Three Put a heaped teaspoon of
mincemeat in each pastry case.
Stamp out nine more, slightly
smaller rounds to cover the pies.
(You may need to scrunch up
pastry trimmings, knead briefly and
roll out again to get all the rounds
you need.) Using small cutters,
cut out stars, trees or other festive
shapes from the centre of
each round.

Four Cover half the pies with the
shapes and the other half with the
pastry rounds with the centres
removed. Brush the pastry tops with
egg white and dust lightly with
caster sugar. They can be frozen at
this stage, uncooked, in the bun
tins, then removed and packed into
freezer bags. (Freeze for up to
3 months.) Bake the pies from frozen
for 18–20 minutes until the pastry is
crisp and golden. Cool in the tins for
5 minutes, then remove and cool
completely on a wire rack. (If you're
not freezing the pies, then bake for
12–15 minutes.)

✱ MERINGUE PIES
Using half the quantity of pastry,
roll and stamp out 12 rounds. Put
a heaped teaspoon of mincemeat
in each case. Whisk one egg white
until stiff, then whisk in 50 g/2 oz
golden caster sugar until the
mixture forms stiff peaks. Spoon a
little meringue on to each pie to
seal in the filling and bake as
before (picture 2). Do not freeze.

✱ MARZIPAN STAR PIES
Make half the pastry to line
12 bun-tin holes. Fill with
mincemeat. Roll out 85 g/3 oz
marzipan and stamp out 12 small
stars or trees. Put on each pie
and bake or freeze as before.
Dust with icing sugar to serve.

✱ SPICE CRUMBLE PIES
Make the pastry without adding
the egg and water. Put a quarter
into another bowl and stir in
2 teaspoons of mixed spice and
50 g/2 oz flaked almonds. Add the
egg yolk and 1 teaspoon of cold
water to the remaining pastry mix,
and stir to form a dough. Roll out
and line 18 bun-tin holes. Fill with
mincemeat, then sprinkle over the
crumble. Bake or freeze as before.

Preparation: 25 minutes
Cooking: 12–15 minutes
Makes: 18

LESLEY WATERS'

Freeze-ahead
Spicy Cigars

Forget traditional sausage rolls – this elegant, lightly spiced version is fabulous at drinks parties or as an instant starter. The cigars freeze easily to keep for Christmas, though as they're so delicious you might like to make double the quantity and enjoy them before then! They're especially good served with a cooling mint raita dip.

Lesley Waters' lively personality makes her a great favourite on *Ready Steady Cook* and *Food and Drink*. Her varied career includes working as head teacher at Leith's School of Food and Wine in London and she is also the author of several cookery books. Lesley has a real talent for creating recipes that are just that bit different – often lighter, spicier and healthier. Her low-fat menus are regularly featured in *Good Food Magazine*.

Preparation: 30 minutes
Cooking: 20 minutes
Makes: 32

FOR THE CIGARS

250 g/9 oz Cumberland sausagemeat

25 g/1 oz ready-to-eat dried apricots,
   finely chopped

8 large filo pastry sheets,
   each 40 × 30 cm/16 × 12 in

1 egg, beaten

sesame seeds and paprika, for sprinkling

mint raita dip and watercress salad to serve

FOR THE SPICY PASTE

2 tablespoons grapeseed or sunflower oil

1 large onion, finely chopped

1 garlic clove, crushed

1 teaspoon ground cardamom

1 teaspoon ground coriander

1 teaspoon allspice

4 teaspoons paprika

1 teaspoon ground ginger

good pinch of cayenne pepper

1 teaspoon salt

freshly ground black pepper

24

One Preheat the oven to 190°C/Gas 5; fan oven: cook from cold at 170°C. Make the spicy paste: heat the oil in a frying pan with a lid. Add the chopped onion and cook covered over a low heat for 5–7 minutes until softened and golden. Add the remaining paste ingredients (picture 1) and season well with black pepper. Turn up the heat and fry for a further 30 seconds (picture 2). Transfer to a blender or small food processor with 2 tablespoons of cold water and whizz until smooth. Set aside. In a bowl, mix together the sausagemeat and apricots.

Two Lay 1 filo sheet on a work surface, top with another filo sheet and cut into 8 rectangles, 10 × 15 cm/4 × 6 in (picture 3). Spread each rectangle with half a teaspoon of spicy paste (picture 4).

Three Take a heaped teaspoon of the sausage and apricot mixture and shape it into a very thin sausage (picture 5). Lay the thin sausage across the bottom shorter edge of the rectangle, then carefully roll up in the pastry (picture 6). Transfer to a baking sheet lined with baking paper.

Four Repeat with the remaining ingredients to give 32 cigars.

Five Brush the cigars with beaten egg (picture 7).

Six Sprinkle with sesame seeds (picture 8). Bake for 15–18 minutes until the pastry is golden and crispy. Sprinkle with a little paprika 2 minutes before the end of cooking time. The cooked cigars are frozen at this stage: allow them to cool. Freeze on

baking sheets until firm, then transfer to freezing bags or a freezerproof container. When you're ready, cook from frozen at 190°C/Gas 5/fan oven 170°C for 20 minutes.

Serve warm or cold with a mint raita dip, watercress salad and a drizzle of olive oil.

✳ MINT RAITA DIP
Grate half a cucumber, then mix with a 200 g tub of Greek yogurt and 3 tablespoons of chopped fresh mint.

Chocolate
Chestnut Log

FOR THE CHOCOLATE LAYER

200 g/8 oz dark chocolate, plus
   50 g/2 oz to decorate

200 g/8 oz unsweetened chestnut
   purée

5 tablespoons icing sugar

50 g/2 oz liquid glucose

425 ml/³/₄ pint double cream

FOR THE VANILLA FILLING

200 ml/7 fl oz double cream

200 ml/7 fl oz ready-made
   custard

25 g/1 oz icing sugar

1 teaspoon vanilla extract

This make-ahead frozen dessert is a rich but light
alternative to Christmas pudding. It's worth using
the best chocolate – the taste will really come
through. You can buy the liquid glucose from
chemists and larger supermarkets. It's sold in clear
jars and once opened keeps for several months.

Preparation: 20 minutes, plus 2 hours
freezing
Serves: 8–10

One Line the base and sides of a 23 × 33 cm/9 × 13 in Swiss roll tin with a sheet of foil. Break up the chocolate and melt three-quarters in a bowl over a pan of hot water or in the microwave on Medium for about 2 minutes. Let the melted chocolate cool a little while you chop the remainder into chunks.

Two In a large bowl, beat the chestnut purée, sugar and glucose until well mixed (a hand-held mixer makes this job easier). Stir in the melted chocolate (picture 1). Whip the cream until stiff, then fold into the mixture, along with the chopped chocolate (picture 2). Spread the mixture evenly over the tin and smooth the top (picture 3). Freeze for 30 minutes until softly set.

Three Make the vanilla filling: whip the cream until stiff, then fold in the custard, sugar and vanilla. Spread evenly over the chocolate layer in the tin (picture 4) and freeze for 1–1 1/2 hours, until the top layer is just firm.

Four Remove from the freezer (if the chocolate layer is too firm to roll up, leave for 10 minutes to soften slightly). Using the foil to help you, roll up from one short end (pictures 5, 6). Freeze the log on the tin, wrapped in foil, for 2 hours or until completely firm.

Five To decorate, break up the 50 g/2 oz chocolate and melt. Using a teaspoon or piping bag, quickly drizzle fine lines back and forth over the log. Freeze

uncovered until the chocolate has set. Wrap in greaseproof paper and overlap foil.

✱ TO SERVE: Remove this dessert from the freezer to the fridge about an hour before serving – by which time it should be soft enough to slice. If you serve iced desserts too cold, some of the flavour will be lost.

Stilton and Walnut Crunchies

A great gift for those who like to linger over the cheese board, or enjoy a special savoury snack with drinks. You can choose just how far ahead to make these biscuits: the dough can be frozen for up to 2 months, then baked once thawed; or it can chill in the fridge for up to one week. Once baked, the biscuits will keep for up to 3 days in an airtight tin in a cool place.

Preparation: 15 minutes
Cooking: 15 minutes
Makes: about 30

225 g/8 oz plain flour

115 g/4 oz butter, cut into pieces, plus extra for greasing

140 g/5 oz Stilton

85 g/3 oz broken walnuts

2 egg yolks

beaten egg, to glaze

coarse salt, for sprinkling

One Put the flour and butter in a food processor and whizz briefly until the mixture resembles fine breadcrumbs. Crumble in 115 g/ 4 oz of the cheese and 50 g/2 oz of the walnuts. Whizz again briefly to mix. Add the egg yolks; whizz to a paste.

Two Preheat the oven to 180°C/Gas 4/fan oven 160°C. Grease 2 baking sheets. Roll out the pastry on a lightly floured surface to about 5 mm/$\frac{1}{4}$ in thick and stamp out 6 cm/$2\frac{1}{2}$ in rounds. Transfer to the baking sheet and prick lightly with a fork. Brush with beaten egg. Crumble the remaining cheese and scatter over the biscuits along with the coarse salt and reserved walnuts. Bake for 15–20 minutes until just golden. Cool on a wire rack.

✱ HOW TO WRAP IN STYLE: A long, narrow wooden box (about 25 cm x 9 cm x 11.5 cm) is just right for stacking biscuits in a neat row. Using pinking shears, cut two pieces of gold tissue paper to line the box, and tie with a gorgeous gold ribbon.

Red Onion and Apricot  Chutney

This fabulous fruity chutney is great with Christmas cold meats and cheeses. Make it now and it will be perfect for Christmas Day cold supper or Boxing Day. It makes a wonderful gift as well, packed into pretty jars, so you could double up the quantities if you like.

Phil Vickery, star of *Ready Steady Cook* and award-winning chef of the Castle Hotel in Taunton, is renowned for using seasonal produce. Whenever possible, he buys locally grown fruit and vegetables, meat from nearby farms and fish in its proper season. He loves bottling things away, particularly when there is a glut of summer fruits. When it comes to Christmas, he likes to use dried fruits and this is his favourite chutney recipe.

1 red chilli

3 medium onions

250 g/9 oz dried apricots, covered
  with cold water and soaked overnight

100 ml/3½ fl oz olive oil

2 teaspoons cumin seeds

4 teaspoons white mustard seeds

2 teaspoons ground turmeric

2 garlic cloves, crushed

2 tablespoons caster sugar

2 teaspoons salt

200 ml/7 fl oz cider vinegar

100 ml/3½ fl oz white wine vinegar

freshly ground black pepper

Preparation: 15 minutes, plus
overnight soaking

Cooking: 40–50 minutes

Makes: 750 g/1 lb 10 oz

One Seed and finely chop the chilli using a small sharp knife. First remove the stalk, then cut the chilli in half down the length. Scrape out the seeds and discard. If you prefer a hotter chutney leave some in (picture 1). Peel and finely chop the onions (picture 2). Drain the apricots and cut into quarters.

Two Heat the oil in a stainless steel pan, then add the cumin, mustard seeds, turmeric, chilli and garlic (picture 3). Stir well, then cook gently for 2 minutes, stirring occasionally – do not allow the spices to burn (picture 4).

Three Add the onions, sugar and salt, and season well with black pepper (picture 5). Cook for a further 5 minutes until the onions have softened. Pour in the two vinegars and bring to the boil, then reduce the heat (picture 6). Add the chopped apricots and simmer gently for about 35–40 minutes until the chutney is thick and chunky. Season with salt and pepper to taste and allow to cool.

Four Spoon the chutney into jars (picture 7) and store in the fridge for about a week to allow the flavours to develop. The chutney will keep for up to 6 weeks stored in a cool place.

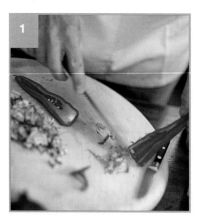

✱ DRIED APRICOTS: You can use ready-to-eat dried apricots, but soaking dried apricots overnight softens them further so they cook more quickly.

✱ PREPARING THE JARS: Use jars with a tight-fitting lid to give you a good seal. Kilner jars are perfect, or you can re-use pickle or jam jars. Check the lid is lined with plastic as the vinegar will react with metal. Preheat the oven to 150°C/Gas2/fan oven 130°C. Wash the jars thoroughly in hot soapy water, then carefully rinse and dry. Lay the jars in the oven for 15 minutes to sterilize, then remove and put on a board to fill them.

FREEZE-AHEAD DINNER PARTY TONY TOBIN'S

Chicken and Clementine Tagine with Couscous

Make this sumptuous dinner party well in advance and freeze it until required – gourmet eating at a moment's notice. On the menu: Tony Tobin's Chicken and Clementine Tagine with Couscous, and Paul Rankin's Chocolate Mousse Cake. To make life even easier, you can divide the preparation over two weeks as suggested here. Make the Tagine one week, and then tackle Paul Rankin's delicious dessert the week after. That way you can spend more time on each dish.

Tony Tobin is well known for his wonderful way with flavour and his light modern approach to food. He doesn't believe in using excess cream in his cooking – his sauces are more likely to be based on flavoured oils, fresh herbs or vegetable purées than rich reduced gravies. This tagine is typical of his no-nonsense style, combining a few seasonal ingredients cooked simply but with care, to produce a delicious main course for a special meal. If you're cooking for four, then the ingredients can easily be halved.

2 onions

4 garlic cloves

2 teaspoons salt

juice of 1 lemon

1 bunch of fresh coriander

2 × 1.5 kg/3 lb 5 oz chickens, each cut into 8 pieces

2 teaspoons freshly ground black pepper

2 teaspoons ground ginger

½ teaspoon saffron filaments

125 ml/4 fl oz olive oil

1 cinnamon stick

12 clementines

350 g/12 oz pitted black olives

450 g/1 lb couscous

Preparation: 45 minutes, plus 30 minutes marinating

Cooking: 1 hour

Serves: 8

One Chop the onions very finely. Peel and crush the garlic.

Two Mix together the garlic, salt and lemon juice and chop half the coriander (picture 1). Add to the mixture, then rub into the chicken pieces in a large bowl (pictures 2, 3).

Three In a bowl, mix together the onions, black pepper, ginger, saffron and olive oil; pour over the chicken. Marinate for 30 minutes. Heat a large flameproof casserole or large pan. Remove the chicken pieces from the marinade, wiping off as much as possible (but don't throw the marinade away). Cook the chicken in batches until golden all over.

Four Return the chicken to the pan, then spoon over the marinade and add enough water to come two-thirds of the way up the chicken (picture 4). Add the cinnamon, bring to the boil, then reduce the heat; simmer for 30 minutes.

Five Wash but don't peel the clementines, then cut each into 8 wedges and add to the mixture (picture 5). Add the olives (picture 6) and simmer for 30 minutes. The dish is frozen at this stage: leave to cool and then transfer to a freezerproof container. (This can be kept frozen for up to 3 months.) To serve, defrost thoroughly, then put in a pan and bring to the boil. Simmer for 25 minutes to thoroughly reheat; continue with next stage.

Six Make the couscous according to the packet instructions (see page 37); keep warm. Remove the chicken from the dish and, if necessary, boil the cooking juices to reduce to a sauce consistency; season. Pour over the chicken.

Seven To serve, spoon the couscous on to a large plate and make a well in the centre. Spoon the chicken, clementines and juices into the middle. Chop the remaining coriander and sprinkle over.

✱ PREPARING AHEAD: If you prefer not to freeze the dish, but still want some time in hand, then the cooked tagine should be cooled quickly, covered and left to chill in the fridge for up to 2 days. Bring gently back to the boil, then cover and keep at simmering point for 20 minutes.

✱ FOR FLAVOUR: Use really good quality olives for this recipe. Buy them loose at the deli counter, so you can taste them first.

✱ PREPARING COUSCOUS: Use quick-cooking couscous, widely available in supermarkets and delis. Tip the couscous into a large bowl and cover with a slightly greater volume of boiling water or stock. The grains need to be covered by at least 5 cm/2 in of water. Leave for 5–10 minutes, then fluff up with a fork and season well. Drizzle with a little olive oil just before serving. If you want to prepare it a little ahead, cook as above, then spread over an ovenproof dish and dot with butter or drizzle with olive oil. Cover the dish with foil and put in a warm oven for 15–20 minutes, after which time it will be even more light and fluffy. Fork up the grains before serving.

Chocolate Mousse Cake

This delectable cake looks absolutely stunning. While it isn't as complicated to make as it looks, it's still quite a challenge with all the techniques involved, so make sure you have the kitchen to yourself and take your time. (And, of course, you can choose your time – this cake freezes beautifully for up to four weeks.)

Paul Rankin is a regular face on TV and, when not showing the rest of us how it's done, he's working in his Belfast restaurant, Roscoff. In fact, this recipe is restaurant standard – and Paul shows you exactly how to make it.

FOR THE BASE

25 g/1 oz icing sugar, plus extra for dusting

50 g/2 oz caster sugar

50 g/2 oz egg whites

4 rounded tablespoons ground almonds, lightly toasted

FOR THE MOUSSE

450 g/1 lb quality plain cooking chocolate, chopped

3 eggs

200 ml/7 fl oz custard (bought or home-made), at room temperature

450 ml/16 fl oz whipping cream

4 tablespoons Cognac or brandy

3 tablespoons finely chopped candied ginger

TO DECORATE

175 g/6 oz plain chocolate

175 g/6 oz white chocolate

single cream, to serve

Preparation: 2 hours, plus 30 minutes freezing

Cooking: 1½ hours

Serves: 10–12

MAKE THE BASE

One Preheat the oven to 120°C/ gas $\frac{1}{2}$; fan oven: cook from cold at 100°C. Line a baking sheet with non-stick baking paper and lightly draw a 20–22 cm/8–8$\frac{1}{2}$ in circle on it as a guide. Have a piping bag with a 1 cm/$\frac{1}{2}$ in plain nozzle ready.

Two Make the base: sift the sugars together into a bowl. In another bowl, whisk the egg whites until stiff. (It is better to use a balloon whisk or hand-held electric whisk as very few mixers can handle such a small amount.) Whisk in a tablespoon of the sugars until firm and glossy. Fold the ground almonds into the rest of the sugar, then carefully fold into the whisked whites with a metal spoon.

Three Put the mixture in the piping bag and pipe the mixture in a continuous spiral to fill the circle – start in the centre and work your way out (picture 1). If it does not reach, use a palette knife to lightly spread it. (It will only be about 1.5 cm/$\frac{1}{2}$ in thick.) Dust the meringue with a little icing sugar, then bake for 1$\frac{1}{2}$ hours until crisp and light golden. Try not to let the meringue get too brown (you may need to change shelves and turn it around in the oven.) Remove from the oven and leave to cool.

✳ TO MAKE A PIPING BAG: Take a 30 cm/12 in square of greaseproof paper and cut in half diagonally to make two triangles. Hold the centre of the longest edge with your finger, then curve one point around to reach the point opposite your finger to form a cone shape. Curve the opposite point until all three points are together. Jiggle them until you have a sharp point where your finger was. Fold over the three points several times to secure, then snip off the end to the required size.

Four Line a 23 cm/9 in spring-form tin with plastic film. Cut two strips of firm plastic, 33 × 7.5 cm/ 13 × 3 in (the kind of firm but flexible clear plastic that you see in document sleeves is fine); use to line the tin sides. Shave a thin layer off the top of the meringue; reserve the shavings. Put the meringue base into the tin.

MAKE THE MOUSSE

One Melt the chocolate in a bowl set over a pan of simmering water (the base of the bowl mustn't touch the water), then set aside to cool for about 15 minutes. Using a hand-held electric whisk, whisk the eggs in a bowl over the simmering water for about 8 minutes until light and fluffy and they leave a trail when the beaters are lifted out. Remove from the heat and whisk until thickened and increased in volume. Slowly whisk in the custard, then fold in the cooled melted chocolate.

Two In a bowl, whip the cream into soft peaks, then fold into the chocolate mixture with the brandy so it has the consistency of softly whipped cream. Divide the mixture evenly between three bowls. Fold the meringue shavings into one mousse, then fold the candied ginger into the second.

Three Pour the meringue mousse on top of the base in the tin and freeze for 10 minutes. Pour over the ginger mousse and freeze for 10 minutes. Finally, pour over the remaining mousse. Cover loosely with plastic film and chill for up to 2 days. The cake is frozen at this stage: open freeze in the tin until firm, then cover with freezer foil or plastic film. When you're ready, proceed with the next stage.

MAKE THE DECORATION

One Use 2 piping bags for the decorations (see tip above on how to make your own). Cut 2 ribbons of greaseproof paper, about 40 × 6 cm/16 × 2½ in, and lay on a baking sheet. Line another baking sheet with greaseproof paper and lightly draw triangles on it, using the template. You'll need 1 triangle per portion, so make about 15 to allow for breakages.

Two Melt the chocolates in separate bowls over two pans of barely simmering water, then put a little of each into two piping bags. Starting with the plain chocolate bag, scribble finely over each paper ribbon, then scribble in the other direction with the white chocolate. If necessary, repeat with each to strengthen the lines. The lines should be fine, but close together to create a filigree (picture 2). Chill until firm.

template

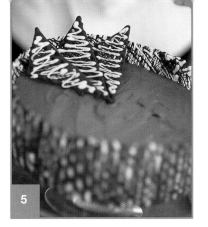

5

Three Pipe a line of plain chocolate around each triangle, then scribble inside with the plain, then the white (picture 3). Chill until firm. When completely chilled, lift them off the paper and pack into a box. They will keep in the fridge for several days. (The ribbons are more fragile, so keep on the tray.)

ASSEMBLE THE CAKE

One Carefully lift off the sides of the tin and peel off the plastic film and strips. Slide the cake on to a flat plate or a cakeboard. Take one chocolate ribbon strip from the fridge and, if too firm, rub the paper lightly with the palm of your hand until it is malleable enough to mould around the side of the cake; press it around the cake (picture 4). Use as much of the second ribbon to cover the remainder of the side of the cake as necessary, trimming off the excess with scissors – leave the paper on the ribbons until the last minute. Chill.

Two To serve, mark each cake portion lightly with a knife. Carefully remove the paper ribbons. Stick a triangle into each portion at a 45 degree angle (picture 5). Dip a long sharp knife into a jug of hot water and dry quickly before slicing. Serve with single cream.

Glazed Ham with
Caramelized Fruits

A glazed ham makes a wonderful centrepiece for a larger party and is one of the traditional dishes we associate with Christmas. This gammon joint is simmered with a clove-studded tangerine and flavourings, then skinned and scored. It is then dowsed with whiskey, studded with stem ginger and brushed with a honey and ginger glaze, before being served with a shallot and tangerine sauce, and caramelized fruits. Serve it hot with simple accompaniments such as creamy mash, red cabbage or leeks. Any leftovers can be served cold with pickles and salads.

**Preparation: 25 minutes, plus
overnight soaking (optional)**

Cooking: $2^{1}/_{2}$–$3^{1}/_{4}$ hours

Serves: 8–10, with leftovers

FOR THE HAM AND GLAZE

2.7–3.6 kg/6–8 lb smoked or unsmoked boned gammon

4 tangerines, clementines or satsumas

15 whole cloves

8 shallots, peeled, left whole or halved if large

3 celery sticks cut into large pieces

6 bay leaves

⅓ bottle (250 ml/9 fl oz) bourbon or Irish whiskey

300 ml/½ pint chicken or ham stock

3 pieces of stem ginger plus 2 tablespoons ginger syrup

50 g/2 oz clear honey plus a little extra

85 g/3 oz demerara sugar

4 fresh figs

bayleaves to garnish

FOR THE SAUCE

4 shallots, peeled and finely chopped

235 g/1 oz butter

2 teaspoons cornflour

100 ml/3½ fl oz tangerine, clementine or
   satsuma juice (about 3 fruits)

squeeze of lemon juice

One Put the gammon in a large pan so it fits snugly. Halve a tangerine, clementine or satsuma and stud with cloves. Add to the pan with the shallots, celery, bay leaves and enough water to cover (picture 1). Bring to the boil, cover and simmer gently for the calculated cooking time (see page 45). Skim off any scum during cooking with a slotted spoon.

Two Remove the gammon from the water and allow to cool slightly, then remove the string. Using a sharp knife, carefully ease away the skin to leave an even layer of fat (picture 2).

Three Using the tip of the knife, score the fat in diagonal lines, one way only, to give a decorative finish. Transfer the scored gammon to a roasting tin.

Four Pour the whiskey all over the gammon (picture 3), then pour the stock into the pan.

Five Preheat the oven to 220°C/Gas 7; fan oven: cook from cold at 200°C. Finely slice the stem ginger and tuck it into the scores of the fat. Mix together the honey, sugar and ginger syrup in a pan and heat gently until slightly thinned. Brush half over the gammon (picture 4). Bake for 15 minutes until beginning to colour.

Six Remove the gammon from the oven and baste with the juices in the roasting tin (picture 5). Glaze with the remaining honey and ginger mixture and bake for a further 15–20 minutes, basting once or twice more, until golden and beginning to char around the edges.

Seven Halve the remaining tangerines, clementines or satsumas and the figs and brush the cut sides with a little honey. Heat a little oil in a frying pan and fry the fruits for about 2–3 minutes on the cut sides until caramelized (picture 6). When the ham is ready, transfer to a warm plate and surround with the fruits and bay leaves; keep warm.

Eight Make the sauce: fry the shallots in the butter for 2 minutes until soft but not brown. Blend the cornflour with a little fruit juice, then stir in the rest. Add the cooking juices to the shallots with the tangerine juice, lemon juice and pepper. Bring to the boil and cook, stirring, for 2 minutes. Serve in a warm sauceboat with the ham.

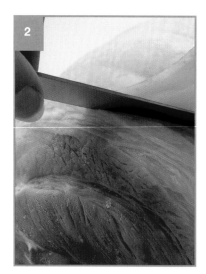

✱ CHOOSING A GAMMON JOINT: Gammon is the hind leg of the bacon pig after curing, but before cooking, and is available smoked or unsmoked – it's down to personal taste. Once cooked, it becomes ham. Allow about 225 g/8 oz raw weight per portion which usually provides plenty of leftovers. The joint should be tied with string when you buy it from the butcher but, if not, tie it yourself before cooking.

✱ DOES IT NEED SOAKING? Soaking removes excess salt. Mild cured gammon shouldn't need soaking, but if in doubt it's best to soak it in cold water for 24 hours before cooking, particularly smoked which tends to be more salty.

✱ CALCULATING THE COOKING TIME: Weigh the gammon joint, then allow 20 minutes cooking time per 450 g/1 lb, plus 20 minutes extra.

✱ WHY SHALLOTS? They have the bouquet of onions without the coarseness. Their sweet, delicate taste makes them useful for adding to sauces.

✱ LEFTOVERS: You can serve glazed ham hot or cold. It will keep in the fridge for up to 5 days for use in sandwiches and salads.

Stilton Rarebit & Chestnut Bubble with Roast Parsnips

This is a vegetarian's dream – a mash of flavoursome winter vegetables, topped with cranberry flavoured parsnips and served with a buttery sauce. This dish freezes well (for up to a month), if you don't want to eat it the same day you make it.

This is a typically inventive dish for Gary. A regular contributor to *Good Food Magazine,* his recipes are always stunning to look at and fabulous to eat. As Gary says, 'This has to be the ultimate vegetarian Christmas dish; it's got just about all the classic British flavours'.

Preparation:	2 hours
Cooking:	1 hour
Serves:	6

FOR THE RAREBIT

225 g/8 oz Stilton, chopped

100 g/4 oz Cheddar, grated

75 ml/3 fl oz milk

25 g/1 oz plain flour

25 g/1 oz fresh white breadcrumbs

½ tablespoon English mustard powder

1–2 shakes balsamic vinegar

1 medium egg, plus 1 medium egg yolk

FOR THE BUBBLE

450 g/1 lb Brussels sprouts, trimmed
   and thinly sliced

2 small onions, thinly sliced

50 g/2 oz butter

115–175 g/4 oz cooked chestnuts,
   chopped (or half 240 g can)

450 g/1 lb cooked potatoes, mashed
   without butter or milk

FOR THE PARSNIPS

25 g/1 oz butter

8–10 medium-sized parsnips
   (1.3–1.8 kg/3–4 lb), peeled,
   quartered lengthways and
   cores removed

3 tablespoons cranberry jelly

FOR THE SAUCE

150 ml/¼ pint reduced vegetable
   stock (either home-made
   or stock cubes)

squeeze of lemon juice

50–85 g/2–3 oz unsalted butter

1 teaspoon each chopped fresh
   parsley, sage and thyme,
   mixed together

✱ FOR FOUR PORTIONS: Use an 18–20 cm/
7–8 in diameter deep loose-bottomed round cake
tin with the base removed. You could also use a
20 cm/8 in baking ring, or even a large dish.

MAKE THE RAREBIT

One Put the Stilton and Cheddar in a pan with the milk. Heat gently until the cheeses have melted (don't let the mixture boil).

Two When the mixture is bubbling gently, add the flour, breadcrumbs and mustard. Cook for a few minutes, stirring over a low heat until the mixture comes away from the sides of the pan. Add the balsamic vinegar and leave to cool.

Three When cold, pour the mixture into a food processor, turn on the motor and slowly add the egg and egg yolk (picture 1). Once the eggs are mixed in, remove from the processor and wrap in plastic film, then put in a polythene bag and chill in the coldest part of the fridge while you prepare the rest of the dish.

MAKE THE BUBBLE

One Blanch the sprouts in boiling salted water for about 1 minute. Drain and refresh in iced water. Line a roasting tin with a double thickness of kitchen paper and put the sprouts in an even layer. Cover with 2 more sheets of kitchen paper and press firmly to dry the sprouts as much as possible.

Two Fry the onions in half the butter for 4–5 minutes until tender in a frying pan. Leave to cool.

Three Add the sprouts and chestnuts to the onions, then add the mashed potatoes a little at a time until the bubble is combined and firm. Season.

Four Liberally grease the cake tin or ring and an ovenproof frying pan with the remaining butter. Put the tin upside-down in the pan (the rim is now at the top so the cake can be removed easily) (picture 2). Spoon the bubble into the tin or ring; then press down. Shallow fry for 5–7 minutes so the base is golden and crisp. Set aside.

COOK THE PARSNIPS

One Preheat the oven to 230°C/Gas 8/fan oven 210°C. Heat the butter in a roasting tin over a moderate heat, then cook the parsnips for 10 minutes until golden. Season, then roast for 25–30 minutes.

Two The parsnips will now be crisp (almost overcooked) and deep golden brown, with a soft and creamy interior. While they are still hot lightly coat them in cranberry jelly.

Three The parsnips can now be packed on top of the bubble; put them end to end in concentric circles, starting at the edge of the ring and working inwards (picture 3). Pack them tightly together so the cake keeps its shape when the ring is removed. The cake can be frozen at this stage: open-freeze the whole dish in the tin before baking. Wrap in freezer film and freeze for up to a month. Defrost overnight in the fridge and continue with the next stage.

TO FINISH

One Preheat the oven to 200°C/Gas 6/fan oven 180°C. Put about two-thirds of the rarebit between two pieces of plastic film and roll into a disc the same diameter as the cake (this can be prepared in advance) (picture 4). Remove the plastic film and sit the rarebit on the cake. Bake in the ovenproof pan for 30 minutes until the cake is heated through and the top is golden brown (meanwhile, make the sauce). Remove the ring and cut into thick wedges. Serve with the herb butter sauce.

MAKE THE SAUCE

One Put the stock, lemon juice and 50 g/2 oz of the butter into a pan and bring to a simmer, whisking. Season. Whisk vigorously to give a light creamy consistency. If the sauce is too thin, then whisk in the remaining butter. Add the herbs just before serving.

✱ USING UP THE RAREBIT: This recipe doesn't use up all the rarebit, but it's difficult to make in a smaller amount because of the egg quantities. Wrap the remainder tightly in plastic film and it will keep in the fridge for up to a week. Use for a special cheese on toast, or put a little on the top of crisply baked slices of French bread and grill until bubbling. Or try a special post-Christmas hot open sandwich. Toast a thick slice of bread. Spread with mayonnaise, cover with slices of turkey and ham if you have it. Spread with cranberry sauce and cover with a thin layer of rarebit. Grill until bubbling and serve with a crisp salad and a glass of sherry. It's also really good on baked potatoes or as a topping for a pasta bake.

Brandy
Butter

Brandy Butter and Cranberry Sauce are quick to make and it is a good idea to get them out of the way now before things really start to hot up in the kitchen.

100 g/4 oz butter, softened

85 g/3 oz caster sugar

50 g/2 oz light muscovado sugar

4 tablespoons brandy

One Beat the butter until it is really soft and light, then beat in the sugars, a little at a time, beating well until the mixture is light and fluffy, about 5 minutes (picture 1).

Two Gradually beat in the brandy (picture 2). Spoon into a dish and rough up the top. Cover with plastic film and store in the fridge for up to 2 weeks.

Serves: 8

Cranberry
Sauce

**225 g/8 oz fresh or frozen
cranberries**

100 g/4 oz sugar

**grated rind and juice of
1 orange**

**glass of port (85–120 ml/
3–4 fl oz)**

One Put the cranberries in a pan with the sugar, the orange rind and juice (picture 1) and the port. Stir over a gentle heat until the sugar has dissolved, then simmer for 5–8 minutes until the cranberries are softened and the sauce has thickened (picture 2).

Two Allow the sauce to cool, then pour it into a rigid container. Keep in the fridge for up to a week or freeze for up to 2 months.

Preparation:	5 minutes
Cooking:	10–12 minutes
Serves:	10–12

Starry
Christmas Cake

700 g/1½ lb white marzipan
(450 g/1 lb if decorating the
top only)
25–28 cm/10–11 in cakeboard
apricot jam
2–3 egg whites
700 g/1½ lb icing sugar (450 g/
1 lb if decorating the top only),
plus extra for dusting
2 tablespoons liquid glucose
(buy from the chemist)
edible silver balls and wide silver
ribbon, to decorate

Your Moist and Fruity Christmas Cake (page 10) should be well matured by now. This easy but dazzling decoration is a fitting crown for it.

Preparation: 30 minutes, plus 2 days drying

★ PREPARING AHEAD: The stars can be made up to 4 weeks before you need them. Allow them to dry completely and store in a food box, interleaved with greaseproof paper.

One Roll out 225 g/8 oz marzipan on a board dusted with icing sugar. Cut out 20–25 stars with small and medium cutters (picture 1); put on a tray lined with baking parchment. Leave for 2 days.

Two Roll out a circle of marzipan to fit the top of the cake – a 20 cm/8 in round cake tin is the best guide (picture 2). To decorate the sides of the cake, cut a strip of baking parchment the same depth and length. Roll out the rest of the marzipan on the paper and trim to fit.

Three Put the cake on the cake board. Brush the top (and sides, if decorating) of the cake with jam (picture 3). Lay the marzipan circle on top (picture 4) (wrap the strip around the side, if using; peel off the paper).

Four Beat the egg whites lightly (2 for the top only, 3 for the top and sides), then gradually sift in the icing sugar, beating all the time until smooth and glossy. Beat in the glucose, then add enough icing sugar to form stiff peaks.

Five Spoon the icing on top of the cake, then swirl it over using a flat-bladed knife (picture 5). Spread it flat on the sides to make tying the ribbon easy.

Six Smear a little icing on the tips of the marzipan stars and stick on the silver balls. Stick the marzipan stars on to the cake (picture 6). Stick a few more silver balls on to the stars if necessary and sprinkle a few over the top of the cake. Leave to set, then tie the ribbon.

Pistachio  Chocolate Brittle

You can vary the nuts, but always use unsalted ones. These chocolates should be kept cool, or chilled, until you're ready to wrap them – they're best eaten within 2–3 weeks.

85 g/3 oz shelled unsalted pistachio nuts

175 g/6 oz milk chocolate

175g /6 oz white chocolate

350 g/12 oz plain chocolate

rice paper

One Cover the pistachios with boiling water and leave for 2 minutes. Drain and rub between sheets of kitchen paper to remove as much skin as possible. Pick off any remaining skin.

Two Roughly chop the milk and white chocolate. Break up 100 g/4 oz of the plain chocolate and melt in a bowl set over a pan of gently simmering water (or microwave on High for about 2 minutes). Remove from the heat.

Three Line the base and part way up the sides of a 20 cm/8 in square baking tin with rice paper. Spread the melted chocolate over the base and scatter with the chopped chocolate and pistachios. Melt the remaining plain chocolate and pour over. Leave to set.

Four Before wrapping, break into jagged pieces using the tip of a sturdy knife.

✱ PRESENTATION: The surface may develop a white bloom, like any chocolate bar – but don't worry. It doesn't affect the taste, and you can disguise it by dusting very lightly with cocoa powder.

✱ HOW TO WRAP IN STYLE: Take a 28 cm/11 in dinner plate with a plain coloured border and write a message using Pebeo Gold Cerne Relief, squeezed straight from the tube. Leave to dry. Arrange the brittle on a plate, overwrap with clear Cellophane and secure in a bunch in the centre with an elastic band.

Preparation: 20 minutes
Makes: about 800 g/1lb 12 oz

Super-rich Chocolate Truffles

An ideal gift for chocoholics – they're quick and easy to make and cheaper than shop-bought varieties. As they use fresh cream, they'll keep for only up to a week in the fridge.

150 ml/¼ pint extra thick double cream

300 g/10 oz good quality plain chocolate with at least 55 per cent cocoa solids, broken into pieces

3 tablespoons brandy, rum, or orange-flavoured liqueur (optional)

cocoa powder, for dusting

One Heat the cream in a pan without boiling; remove from the heat and stir in the chocolate. Leave for 2–3 minutes, then stir until melted and smooth. Stir in the spirit or liqueur, if using, and pour into a bowl. Chill until firm (about 2 hours).

Two Dust your hands with cocoa and shape teaspoonsful of the mixture into small balls. Roll in more cocoa, then wrap in foil to protect.

✱ VARY THE FLAVOUR:
For amaretti truffles, finely crush 50 g/2 oz amaretti biscuits. Stir into the cream and chocolate with 2 tablespoons Amaretto liqueur. Roll in crushed amaretti biscuits instead of cocoa.

✱ HOW TO WRAP IN STYLE:
For a simple pyramid box, to hold five foil-wrapped truffles overwrapped in tissue paper, take a 25 cm/10 in square of metallic card (from art shops). Score a central square measuring 7 cm/22¾ in for the base. Mark out 4 triangles from each side of the base. Cut around the triangles, then put the truffles on the base. Fold up the sides into a pyramid, punch a hole in the top of each triangle and tie with sparkly string; add a matching triangular-shaped tag.

Preparation: 20 minutes

Neapolitan Festive Ring (Struffoli di Napoli)

Antonio has fond memories of childhood Christmases when the family gathered round the table to make these sweet delicacies, nicknamed 'poor man's hazelnuts'. The finished ring is sure to impress friends and family. As Antonio says, 'If Neapolitans can't celebrate Easter without the *pastiera* – the Easter cake – it's even more unthinkable to celebrate Christmas without *struffoli*.'

Antonio is a much-loved TV cook, and the author of many top-selling books. *Antonio Carluccio's Italian Feast* won him a *Good Food* award for Favourite Cookery Book in 1997.

FOR THE DOUGH

5 medium eggs

3 tablespoons sugar

450 g/1 lb type 00 flour

grated rind of 1 lemon

grated rind of 1 orange

pinch of salt

1 tablespoon pure alcohol (if not available, use a strong vodka)

oil, for deep frying

FOR THE CARAMEL

½ orange and ½ lemon

250 g/9 oz orange blossom honey (about ½ jar)

100 g/4 oz sugar

FOR THE DECORATION

edible silver balls, silver leaf, angelica or candied peel (optional)

Preparation: 30 minutes, plus 2 hours resting

Cooking: 8–10 minutes

Serves: 10

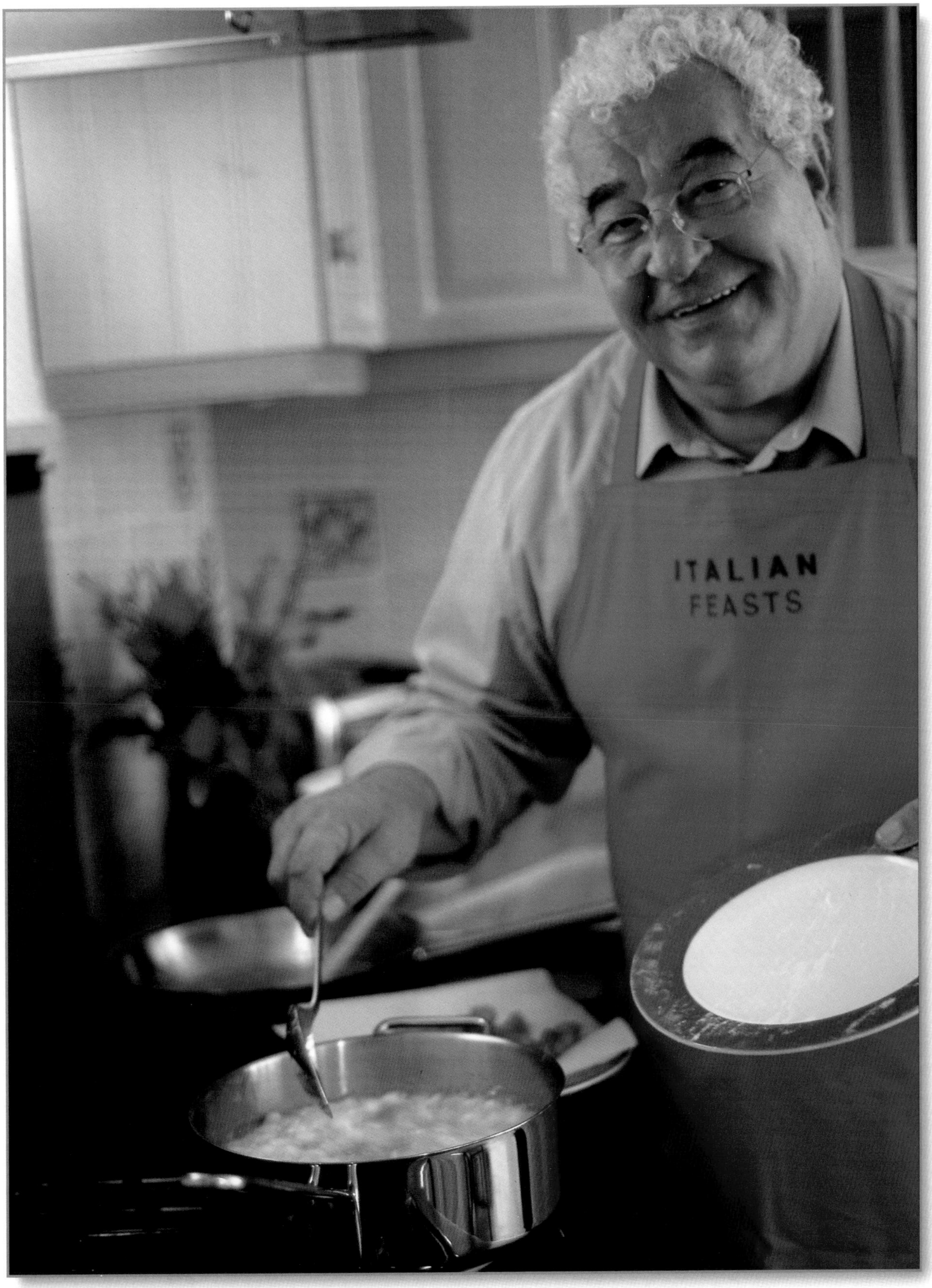
ITALIAN
FEASTS

One Make the dough for the *struffoli*: beat the eggs and sugar in a bowl. Mix in flour, citrus rind, salt and alcohol. Knead for 3–4 minutes (picture 1). Shape into a ball; cover and rest it for 2 hours in a cool place.

Two Take a little bit of the dough at a time and, using your hands, roll into sausage shapes about 1 cm/½ in in diameter (picture 2). Cut each sausage into pieces about the size of a hazelnut (picture 3). This is laborious so get friends and family to help. Toss the pieces of dough in a fine sprinkling of flour to stop them sticking (picture 4).

Three Pour some oil into a pan to a depth of about 2.5 cm/1in. Heat the oil and fry the *struffoli* for about 2–3 minutes until lightly brown and puffed up (picture 5) (do in batches). Remove with a slotted spoon. Drain on kitchen paper. Continue until all dough has been used.

Four Make the caramel: pare the rind from the orange and lemon (avoid any white pith) and cut into fine shreds. Put the honey and sugar in a heavy-based pan with 2 tablespoons of water. Heat gently until the liquid becomes clear. Add the shredded rinds, bring to the boil and simmer for a few minutes to make a light syrup. Add the *struffoli* (picture 6). Stir carefully until they are coated in syrup.

Five Arrange the *struffoli* in a ring on the plate.

Six Sprinkle with silver balls, silver leaf and angelica or candied peel, if using; leave to cool. The *struffoli* will keep in the syrup for up to a week in a polythene container with a lid. Store in a cool place.

✴ TYPE 00 OR DOPPIO ZERO FLOUR: This is superfine flour, sold in Italian delis and larger supermarkets, which gives the dough a light texture.

✴ USING THE RIGHT HONEY: Orange or lemon blossom, or acacia, gives the best flavour.

Canapés without Tears

There's nothing more fiddly and time-consuming than making traditional canapés. Baking the classic array of mini-pastries, biscuits, baby quiches and puffs can take a whole day, and though they look beautiful and certainly show the skill (and patience) of the cook, there's an easier way that tastes just as good. Hence this fuss-free canapé guide, with just four basics – toasts, pastries, baby roast potatoes and chips – each transformed into something special, with mainly storecupboard ingredients.

Serve cold canapés first, then move on to hot. Finish with the chunky chips – they're irresistible. If you make the whole selection, you'll have enough for a drinks party for ten guests – though the recipes can easily be multiplied for larger gatherings. Some can be made ahead, some at the last minute – whatever suits you.

Timeplan for a 6.30pm drinks party

THE DAY BEFORE:

Make the toasts for the crostini; cool and store in an airtight container. Make the salsa; cover and chill.

ON THE DAY:

4.30pm

Make the Quick Guacamole and Herby Fromage Frais dips; cover and chill. Make the Mini Roast Potatoes; cool.

5.30pm

Prepare and cook the oven chips. Prepare the Savoury Puff Squares, but don't bake them; cover and chill. Remove chilled items from the fridge. Top all the crostini except the Prawn and Tomato Salsa.

JUST BEFORE SERVING:

Halve and put toppings on the potatoes (warm them first if you like). Top the Prawn and Tomato Crostini. Grill the Blue Cheese Mini Potatoes. Cook the Savoury Puffs at intervals during the evening.

Children are the best waiters on these occasions – but failing that, recruit a couple of friends as it's vital to keep nibbles moving.

Savoury Puff Squares

These are little pastry squares with four different toppings – if you're making bigger batches, cook each topping in succession while the last lot is being scoffed.

Preheat the oven to 200°C/ Gas 6/fan oven 180°C. Cut a 500 g packet of puff pastry in half and roll one half out to a 15 cm/ 6 in square. (Wrap the other half in plastic film and freeze for use in another recipe.) Trim slightly to straighten the edges, then cut into 16 small squares. Transfer to a lightly greased baking sheet. Add the toppings (see right) and bake for 10–15 minutes until the pastry is puffed and golden.

Preparation: 30–40 minutes
Cooking: 10–15 minutes
Makes: 16 puffs

THE TOPPINGS

✱ PEPPER AND PARMESAN
Divide 2 tablespoons of mixed pepper antipasti (from a jar) between 4 pastry squares. Sprinkle with a little black pepper and grated Parmesan.

✱ MUSHROOM AND MOZZARELLA
Divide 2 tablespoons of mixed mushroom antipasti (from a jar) between 4 pastry squares. Sprinkle 1 tablespoon of chopped fresh parsley and 25 g/1 oz mozzarella between the squares and season with a little black pepper.

✱ SPICY SAUSAGE AND SPINACH
Thaw 25 g/1 oz frozen leaf spinach, then squeeze out the excess moisture. Divide the spinach, 25 g/1 oz sliced chorizo sausage and 1 tablespoon of pine nuts between 4 pastry squares. Just before baking, drizzle over a little olive oil.

✱ TOMATO AND GOAT'S CHEESE
Roughly chop 1 small tomato, then divide between 4 pastry squares. Sprinkle with 25 g/1 oz crumbled goat's cheese.

Mini
Roast Potatoes

Small or baby potatoes are ideal for roasting and topping; served warm as canapés, they're truly tasty. You can cook the potatoes up to 2 hours ahead, but don't cut them in half. Let them cool completely, then cover and store in the fridge. Warm through before serving or serve at room temperature.

Preheat the oven to 190°C/Gas 5; fan oven: cook from cold at 170°C. Toss 8 small potatoes in 2 tablespoons of olive oil and tip into a roasting tin. Sprinkle with coarse sea salt and freshly ground black pepper, then roast for 30–40 minutes until tender. Leave the potatoes to stand until they are cool enough to handle, then split them in half lengthways.

Preparation: 30 minutes
Cooking: 30–40 minutes
Makes: 16 mini potatoes

THE TOPPINGS

✱ INSTANT CORONATION CHICKEN
Combine 25 g/1 oz roughly chopped cooked chicken and 1 tablespoon of chopped red pepper. Stir in 2 tablespoons of fromage frais, 1 teaspoon of curry paste, 2 teaspoons of mango chutney and 1 tablespoon of chopped parsley. Spoon on to 4 potatoes. Chill until needed.

✱ BLUE CHEESE AND CHIVES
Crumble 25 g/1 oz blue cheese and divide between 4 potato halves. Sprinkle over 1 tablespoon of chopped chives. Before serving, grill for 1–2 minutes until bubbling.

✱ SMOKED SALMON AND HORSERADISH
Mix 1 teaspoon of horseradish sauce with 1 tablespoon of crème fraîche and divide between 4 potato halves. Tear 25 g/1 oz smoked salmon into 8 pieces and put 2 on top of each potato half. Cover and chill until needed.

✱ CRÈME FRAÎCHE AND SPRING ONION
Season 2 tablespoons of crème fraîche with salt and pepper, then divide between 4 potato halves. Chop 2 spring onions, sprinkle over the potatoes, cover and chill. Just before serving, sprinkle with freshly ground black pepper.

Quick Crostini

One small French stick is all you need to make the base of these easy nibbles. Look out for the thin French sticks rather than the traditional size, as they slice into the perfect-sized rounds for canapés. If you like, make the toasts the day before and cool completely; pack in an airtight container.

Preheat the oven to 190°C/Gas 5/fan oven 170°C. Cut a thin French stick into 16 slices about 5 mm/¼ in thick. Lay on a baking sheet and drizzle over 1–2 tablespoons of olive oil. Bake for 10 minutes until light golden.

Preparation: 5 minutes
Cooking: 10 minutes
Makes: 16 crostini

THE TOPPINGS

✱ PRAWN AND TOMATO SALSA
Spoon a teaspoon each of the Easy Tomato Salsa (see page 65) on 4 of the toasts (no more than 10 minutes before serving or the toast will go soggy). Put a cooked tiger prawn on top of each; garnish each with a coriander leaf.

✱ PROSCIUTTO AND PEAR
Cut half a small pear into tiny dice and toss with 1 tablespoon of crème fraîche. Divide between 4 toasts. Tear 1 slice of prosciutto into 4 pieces and put on top of the pear mixture.

✱ FESTIVE TURKEY AND CRANBERRY
Divide 2 tablespoons of cranberry sauce between 4 toasts and spread not quite to the edges. Divide 25 g/1 oz chopped cooked turkey between the toasts and top each with a dollop of cranberry sauce. Sprinkle over snipped chives to garnish.

Chunky Oven Chips
and Dips

Chunky chips are the in thing – they are unfailingly popular as guests enjoy a second or third drink, especially when served with a selection of tasty dips.

MAKE THE CHIPS

Preheat the oven to 200°C/Gas 6; fan oven: cook from cold at 180°C. Scrub 4 175 g/6 oz potatoes and cut each into 8 wedges. Transfer to a roasting tin and drizzle over 3 tablespoons of olive oil. Season well, then sprinkle a good pinch of hot chilli powder over half of the potatoes and bake for 40–50 minutes, turning occasionally.

Preparation: 15 minutes	
Cooking: 40–50 minutes	
Serves: 10	

VARY THE FLAVOURS

✱ ROSEMARY CHIPS: Sprinkle 1 tablespoon of chopped fresh rosemary over the potatoes before roasting.

✱ GARLIC CHIPS: Sprinkle over 3 finely chopped garlic cloves before roasting.

✱ LEMONY CHIPS: Tuck in lemon wedges between the potatoes before roasting.

The Dips

EASY TOMATO SALSA

A simple, not too spicy salsa that's not only served as a dip but is also used as a topping for the Prawn and Tomato Crostini and as a base for the Guacamole. If you like a spicier salsa, simply add another chilli. It can be made the day before you need it, kept covered and chilled.

Tip a 400 g can of chopped tomatoes in rich tomato juice into a food processor. Throw in a roughly chopped red chilli, 2 roughly chopped tomatoes, a small bunch of coriander, 2 garlic cloves, the rind and juice of 1 lime and 1 teaspoon of caster sugar. Whizz for about 20 seconds; taste and season. Cover and chill until needed.

Preparation: 10 minutes
Serves: 10

HERBY FROMAGE FRAIS

This refreshing dip uses a mixture of fresh parsley, dill, coriander and chives, but you can use whatever herbs you have to hand.

Mix 4 tablespoons of roughly chopped fresh herbs with 2 200 g tubs of fromage frais. Season lightly, cover and chill until needed (it can be made up to 2 hours ahead).

Preparation: 5 minutes
Serves: 10

QUICK GUACAMOLE

If you've made the salsa, you'll already have done most of the work for this dip – it's simply a case of whizzing it in the food processor with an avocado.

Halve, stone and peel a large ripe avocado, roughly chop the flesh and tip into a food processor. Spoon in 5 tablespoons of the Easy Tomato Salsa and whizz to a chunky purée. Transfer the guacamole to a small serving bowl and squeeze over the juice of 1 lime to prevent discoloration. Cover and chill until needed (it can be made up to 2 hours ahead).

Preparation: 5 minutes
Serves: 10

Jewelled
Madeira Cakes

FOR THE CAKE

350 g/12 oz butter, softened

350 g/12 oz caster sugar

6 medium eggs

425 g/15 oz self-raising flour

1 tablespoon baking powder

1 tablespoon vanilla essence

finely grated rind of 2 oranges,
   plus 2 tablespoons juice

FOR THE DECORATION

200 g/8 oz apricot jam

1 kg/2 lb 4 oz yellow
   marzipan

300 g/10 oz icing sugar,
   plus extra

6 tablespoons Cointreau or
   other orange-flavoured
   liqueur

250 g/9 oz luxury glacé fruits

waxed or greaseproof paper
   and thin string

Preparation: 1 hour
Cooking: 1 hour
Makes: 4 cakes about 13 cm/5 in
square

These exquisite mini-cakes – buttery Madeira wrapped in almond paste and steeped in a liqueur glaze – make beautiful gifts. They only keep for up to a week, so think ahead when you want to give them.

One Preheat the oven to 160°C/Gas 3/fan oven 150°C. Grease and line a 23 cm/9 in square cake tin. Beat together all the cake ingredients in a large bowl until creamy. Spoon into the tin, level the top and bake for about 1 hour until just firm and a skewer pushed into the centre comes out clean. Leave to cool in the tin.

Two Prepare the decoration: melt the jam in a pan over a medium heat, then press through a sieve. Peel the paper away from the cake and cut into four squares. (If the cake is domed, slice off the top to level.) Brush the sides with the glaze.

Three For each cake, thinly roll a quarter of the marzipan on a surface lightly dusted with icing sugar. Cut out 4 oblongs 1 cm/ ½ in taller than the cake itself. Press against the sides, making sure they stand above the cake top. Pinch together at the corners.

Four Beat together the icing sugar and liqueur to make a thin glaze. Spoon over half to flood the tops of the cakes. Decorate each with a few pieces of glacé fruit, then drizzle over the remaining glaze. Leave to set.

Five Wrap the cakes in 2 strips of waxed or greaseproof paper, to line the base and sides. Tie with string.

✱ HOW TO WRAP IN STYLE: Cut a 14 cm/5½ in square of thick card to support the base. Stand a cake on top and wrap with greaseproof paper or white tissue, then overwrap with cotton fabric. Secure with 2 lengths of satin ribbon, 60 cm/24 in long, knotted in the centre.

Festive
Almond Biscuits

These are light biscuits with a surprise almond filling and orange-scented sugar. They'll keep for up to a week in an airtight container, or freeze for up to 2 months.

Preparation: 30 minutes
Cooking: 20 minutes
Makes: 20

75 g/3 oz unsalted butter, chilled and cut into pieces, plus extra

115 g/4 oz self-raising flour

75 g/3 oz ground almonds

100 g/4 oz caster sugar

50 g/2 oz marzipan, cut into 20 cubes

2 oranges

50 g/2 oz icing sugar

One Put the butter in a food processor with the flour and almonds. Whizz to fine breadcrumbs. Add half the caster sugar; whizz until the mixture starts to cling together, then work lightly into a ball with your hands.

Two Thinly roll out half of the dough between two pieces of plastic film on a lightly floured surface. Use a 6 cm/2½ in cutter to cut out crescents; put 10 on a greased baking sheet. Roll half the marzipan into sausages and lay on the crescents. Top each with another crescent (reroll trimmings if necessary) and seal the edges.

Three Make stars with remaining dough and marzipan. Chill for 30 minutes. Preheat the oven to 160°C/Gas 3/fan oven 150°C. Pare strips of orange rind, put on a baking sheet and bake for 3 minutes to dry slightly; cool. Mix the remaining caster sugar and the icing sugar; toss with the rind.

Four Bake biscuits for 18–20 minutes; cool on a wire rack. Gently toss in a little of the orange sugar and pack; sprinkle with the remaining sugar.

✱ HOW TO WRAP IN STYLE: Decorate a terracotta pot with Magic Leaf. Use the bonding agent to paint on simple designs; leave for 15 minutes, then rub on the gold leaf. Push a square of metallic organza into the pot, fill with biscuits and tie with cord.

AINSLEY HARRIOTT'S

Roast Pork
with Chilli Mango Stuffing

Ainsley is a great friend of *Good Food* – he was the magazine's TV Personality of the Year in 1997 and 1998. He came up with this alternative roast for the Christmas table – a delicious stuffed pork dish – using lots of his favourite flavours such as chilli, lime and mango to make a wonderfully exuberant stuffing. The beauty of this dish is that it can be completely prepared the day before cooking and leftovers can be served cold with a big salad.

Preparation: 40 minutes, plus 2 hours marinating

Cooking: 45 minutes–1 hour

Serves: 6–8

FOR THE PORK AND MARINADE

1.8 kg/4 lb piece boned pork loin, scored

3 limes

2 garlic cloves

2 tablespoons soy sauce

3 tablespoons olive oil

5 cm/2 in piece root ginger

FOR THE STUFFING

225 g/8 oz day-old white bread, broken up

25 g/1 oz butter

4 tablespoons olive oil, plus extra for brushing

1 large red chilli, finely chopped

2.5 cm/1 in piece root ginger, grated

bunch of spring onions, sliced

1 glass white wine

large pinch ground allspice

100 g/4 oz dried mango slices

bay leaves, to garnish (optional)

FOR THE GRAVY

150 ml/¼ pint chicken or vegetable stock

sea salt and freshly ground black pepper

One Make the marinade: grate the rind from 2 of the limes and squeeze the juice from all 3. Finely chop the garlic and grate the ginger (picture 1).

Two Put the lime rind and juice, garlic and ginger in a bowl and stir in the soy sauce and olive oil.

Three Pour the marinade into a shallow non-metallic dish that is large enough to take the pork comfortably (picture 2). Add the pork, skin-side up (picture 3); cover with plastic film. Marinate in the fridge for at least 2 hours.

Four Preheat the oven to 230°C/Gas 8; fan oven: cook from cold at 210°C. Make the stuffing: whizz the bread to crumbs in a food processor.

Five Heat the butter and 2 tablespoons of oil in a frying pan (picture 4). Fry the chilli and ginger for 1 minute, stirring. Tip in the crumbs and fry over a fairly high heat for 4–5 minutes, tossing occasionally until golden (picture 5). Add the spring onions, wine and allspice and cook for 1 minute. Season, remove from the heat and leave to cool slightly.

Six Remove the pork from the marinade and dry the skin with kitchen paper; reserve the marinade. Cut a horizontal slice into the pork, open it out and lay the mango slices inside, then spoon on as much of the stuffing as you can. Bring up the sides of the meat to put it back together, and tie with string at 2.5 cm/1 in intervals (pictures 6 and 7).

Seven Wrap remaining stuffing in a foil parcel. Brush the pork skin lightly with olive oil and sprinkle evenly with sea salt.

Eight Heat the remaining oil in a roasting tin over a medium heat. Add the pork and sear all over until golden (picture 8) then roast for 20 minutes. Reduce to 190°C/Gas 5/ fan oven 170°C and cook for 45 minutes–1 hour.

Nine Transfer the pork to a chopping board and leave it to rest for 5–10 minutes. Put the roasting tin over a medium heat, pour in the reserved marinade and stock. Bring to the boil and simmer for 4–5 minutes until reduced by about a third. Slice the pork thickly (picture 9) and serve with gravy. Garnish with bay leaves, if liked.

✱ PREPARING AHEAD: Make the stuffing and leave to cool. When cold, stuff the pork and tie into a neat shape. Wrap in foil and store in the fridge for up to 2 days. Bring back to room temperature before roasting.

✱ COOKING WITH GINGER: If you use ginger in cooked dishes there's no need to peel it first as the skin will soften as it cooks.

✱ DRIED MANGO: This is sold in packets in the dried fruits and nuts section of the supermarket.

✱ PERFECT CRACKLING: Leg or loin joint is best for this. Get your butcher to score the skin for you about 1 cm/½ in apart (the finer the scoring, the crispier the crackling). Dry the skin, brush with a little oil and sprinkle with sea salt.

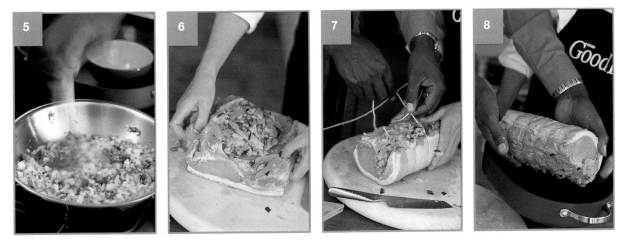

ANTONY WORRALL THOMPSON'S

Fabulous Ways
with Vegetables

If you're cooking a traditional turkey but want to serve some unusual veggie accompaniments, who better to work some magic than Antony Worrall Thompson? Everyone might expect Brussels sprouts – but Antony transforms these and other seasonal vegetables into something really special.

As well as making regular appearances on *Ready Steady Cook* , Antony is resident chef on *Food and Drink*. He also runs two highly-acclaimed restaurants with his wife, Jacinta.

Broccoli and
Leek Purée

85 g/3 oz unsalted butter

**700 g/1 lb 9 oz leeks,
washed and shredded**

**1 teaspoon soft fresh thyme
leaves**

**225 g/8 oz potatoes, peeled
and quartered**

**450 g/1 lb broccoli, stems
sliced and florets separated**

142 ml carton double cream

One Melt the butter in a large pan over a medium heat. Add the leeks and thyme. Cover, reduce the heat and cook for 15–20 minutes until the leeks are very soft.

Two Meanwhile, cook the potatoes in boiling salted water for 10–12 minutes until almost tender. Add the broccoli stems and cook for 5 minutes; add the florets and cook for 3 minutes more until tender.

Three Drain the potatoes and broccoli well and transfer to a food processor with the leeks. Process until smooth (you may have to do this in batches). Return the purée to a clean pan. Stir in the cream (picture 1), season and reheat gently just before serving.

✱ PREPARING AHEAD: Shred the leeks and trim the broccoli. Store in separate polythene bags in the fridge for up to a day. You could cook the dish beforehand, cool it and chill in the fridge for up to a day; then reheat it gently when required.

Preparation: 15 minutes
Cooking: 20 minutes
Serves: 6–8

Mushrooms and Chestnuts
in Cream

50 g/ 2 oz unsalted butter

700 g/1lb 9 oz chestnut
  mushrooms, quartered

6 tablespoons dry sherry

1 onion, finely chopped

1 teaspoon soft fresh thyme
  leaves

300 ml/½ pint chicken stock

142 ml carton double cream

450 g/1lb cooked whole
  chestnuts

One Melt half the butter in a heavy-based frying pan. Add the mushrooms (picture 1) and cook over a high heat, tossing occasionally, for 6–8 minutes until golden. Add the sherry and cook for a few minutes more until reduced. Remove from the pan; keep warm.

Two Heat the remaining butter in the same pan and add the onion and thyme. Cook over a medium heat for 3 minutes without browning. Pour in the chicken stock and simmer for 6 minutes.

Three Return the mushrooms to the pan (picture 2), stir in the cream and warm through. Fold in the chestnuts and season to taste. Warm through again to serve.

✱ PREPARING AHEAD: You can make the dish a few hours in advance, but don't add the chestnuts. Add them and warm through just before serving.

✱ BUYING CHESTNUTS: Cooked whole chestnuts are available from larger supermarkets, either vacuum packed or canned. For this recipe, you will need a 450 g vacuum pack or two 300 g cans.

Preparation:	10 minutes
Cooking:	20 minutes
Serves:	6–8

Corn
Pudding

25 g/1 oz unsalted butter

5 rashers streaky bacon,

   cut into thin strips

450 g/1 lb leeks,

   washed and shredded

1 red pepper, seeded

   and diced

3 corn cobs or

   300 g/10 oz frozen

2 tablespoons chopped

   fresh parsley

3 egg yolks

1 teaspoon prepared

   English mustard

600 ml/1 pint double cream

4 drops of Tabasco

splash of Worcestershire

   sauce

One Preheat the oven to 180°C/Gas 4; fan oven: cook from cold at 160°C. Melt the butter in a large pan over a medium heat. Add the bacon and cook for 2–3 minutes until crisp. Add the leeks and pepper and simmer for 3 minutes until any liquid has evaporated. Season to taste; stir in the corn and parsley. Put in a 1.2 litre/2 pint ovenproof dish.

Two In a bowl, whisk together the egg yolks, mustard and cream. Stir in the Tabasco and Worcestershire sauce. Pour over the corn mixture and bake for 45 minutes until golden and just set. Leave to cool for 10 minutes before serving.

✱ PREPARING AHEAD: This dish reheats well, and can be made a few hours in advance. Just before serving, reheat it in a 160°C/Gas 3/fan oven 140°C for 20–30 minutes.

✱ PREPARING CORN ON THE COB: Hold the corn upright on a board. Using a large sharp heavy knife, slice down through the cob to remove the niblets (picture 1). Turn the cob and repeat until all the niblets are removed. Cook for 5 minutes in boiling water, then drain and use. Do not add salt to the cooking water as this toughens the corn.

Preparation: 40 minutes
Cooking: 45 minutes
Serves: 6–8

Christmas
Brussels

450 g/1 lb Brussels sprouts,
   trimmed

85 g/3 oz unsalted butter

1 small onion, finely
   chopped

½ teaspoon fennel seeds

grated rind of 1 orange

½ teaspoon soft fresh
   thyme leaves

175 g/6 oz cooked
   chestnuts, halved

One Cook the sprouts in a pan of boiling salted water for 6 minutes.

Two Heat the butter in a frying pan. Add the onion, fennel seeds, orange rind and thyme and cook for a few minutes until the onions start to colour (picture 1).

Three Tip in the drained sprouts and chestnuts (picture 2) and fry until the sprouts are slightly tinged with brown. Season to taste and serve at once.

✱ PREPARING AHEAD: Trim sprouts and store in a polythene bag in the fridge for up to 2 days. If you want to cook the sprouts ahead, drain them after boiling and plunge them into iced water; then drain again and chill. (This stops cooking and sets the colour.)

✱ COOKING YOUR OWN CHESTNUTS: The easiest way is to put six on a plate, split each and cook on High in the microwave for 1 minute. Continue until all are cooked, then peel and use. Alternatively, split them and bake in a moderate oven for 15–20 minutes before peeling.

Preparation: 20 minutes
Cooking: 15 minutes
Serves: 6

Turkey and all
the Trimmings

To help the big day go smoothly for you –
we have included a shopping list of key
ingredients (page 96), while my timeplan
(opposite) will help you stay calm.

Buttery lemon and lime add a zesty twist to
the traditional turkey, while accompaniments
also get wonderful flavour boosts.

On the menu

- BUTTER-BASTED LEMON AND LIME TURKEY

- CHESTNUT-STUFFED RED ONIONS

- ROSEMARY AND GARLIC ROASTIES

- SAUSAGEMEAT AND THYME KOFTAS

- HONEY MUSTARD PARSNIPS

- PORT AND ORANGE GRAVY

- CRANBERRY SAUCE (SEE PAGE 51)

- BREAD SAUCE

Timeplan for a 2pm lunch

THE DAY BEFORE

Make and chill lemon and lime butter for turkey
Make turkey stock; chill
Make the koftas, wrap in foil and chill
Stuff red onions, cover; keep in a cool place

ON THE DAY

8.30am

Preheat the oven
Butter the turkey breast and truss

9am

Put turkey in to roast
Prepare parsnips and potatoes for the oven

10am

Baste turkey with the pan juices every $\frac{1}{2}$ hour
Infuse milk for bread sauce

12.30pm

Put potatoes in oven
Cook onions

1.00pm

Remove foil from turkey; cover breast with bacon

1.30pm

If turkey is cooked, put on a platter; cover with foil
Put koftas in oven
Make gravy

2pm

Serve lunch: enjoy!

Butter-basted
Lemon and Lime Turkey

The problem of dry breast meat is neatly solved by sliding a layer of lemon and lime butter under the skin, while the comprehensive roasting chart given on page 93 will ensure the cooking time is just right.

1 lemon

1 lime

85 g/3 oz softened butter

5.6 kg/12 lb oven-ready turkey, thawed if frozen

1 onion

225 g/8 oz streaky bacon

bay leaves and thyme sprigs, to garnish

Preparation: 30 minutes

Cooking: time varies according to size of bird

Serves: 10–12

One Grate the rind from the citrus fruits, reserving the flesh. In a bowl, mix together the butter, lemon and lime rinds and season. Spread the butter over a sheet of foil big enough to cover the area of the turkey breast (picture 1). Cover with another sheet of foil and press down to make an even layer of butter. Chill until firm.

Two Preheat the oven to 180°C/Gas 4; fan oven: cook from cold at 160°C. Remove the giblets from the turkey (reserve for the stock and gravy) and wash the bird inside and out. Dry well with kitchen paper. Quarter the lemon and lime, peel and halve the onion. Put these in the cavity of the bird.

Three Loosen the skin of the breast by sliding your hands (take off rings first) between the flesh and the skin – not a pleasant job, but worth doing. Peel the foil from the chilled butter (keep one piece of foil for step 4) then slide it between the breast and skin (picture 2) (it will break up a bit but this is easier than spreading soft butter). Smooth the skin back over the butter then season the turkey generously inside and out. Tie the legs together at the top of the drumsticks to give the turkey a neat shape.

Four Weigh the bird to calculate the cooking time – allow 20 minutes per 450 g/1 lb, plus 20 minutes extra (see page 93). Put the turkey in a dry roasting tin and loosely cover the breast with a sheet of the buttered foil (picture 3). Do not enclose the whole turkey in foil.

Five Roast the turkey for the calculated cooking time, basting with the pan juices every 30–40 minutes. Half an hour before the end of cooking, remove the foil to crisp the skin, baste with the pan juices and lay the bacon in a lattice over the breast (picture 4).

Six To test if the turkey is cooked, pierce the thigh with a skewer at the thickest part. If the juices run clear it is done; if they are a little pink, give it 15 minutes more, then test again. Transfer to a serving platter and cover tightly with foil; rest for 15 minutes to make carving easier.

Seven Spoon off as much fat as possible from the tin, then measure out 175 ml/6 fl oz of the remaining pan juices to make the gravy (page 90); arrange the Chestnut-stuffed Red Onions, and Sausagemeat and Thyme Koftas around the bird and garnish with bay and thyme.

✱ MAKING TURKEY STOCK: Rinse the giblets and put them in a pan with a quartered onion, chopped celery stick, chopped carrot, a few black peppercorns, teaspoon of salt, bay leaf and parsley sprig. Cover with 850 ml/ 1½ pints water and bring to the boil. Skim off any scum, then reduce the heat and partly cover. Simmer for 1 hour then strain.

✱ PREPARING AHEAD: Make this stock up to 2 days ahead. Cool it quickly, then cover and put in the fridge until ready to use. Any left over can be frozen for up to 3 months.

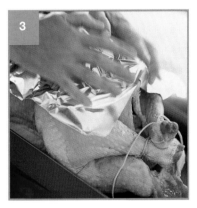

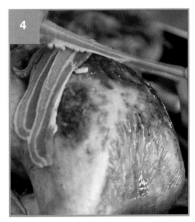

Chestnut-stuffed
Red Onions

6 medium red onions

3 tablespoons olive oil,
plus extra

1 tablespoon balsamic
vinegar

1 celery stick, finely
chopped

1 garlic clove, finely
chopped

85 g/3 oz fresh or frozen
cranberries

200 g/8 oz cooked peeled
chestnuts, finely chopped

25 g/1 oz chopped fresh
parsley or coriander

One Preheat the oven to 180°C/Gas 4/fan oven 160°C. Peel the onions (keep the root intact), and cut each one in half through the middle. Remove several layers from the centre of each half using a teaspoon and a sharp knife (picture 1). Cover any holes in the bottom with a small slice of onion. Finely chop half the removed onion layers (use the rest another time).

Two Arrange the onion halves, cut-side up, in one layer in an oiled ovenproof dish. Whisk together 2 tablespoons of the oil with the balsamic vinegar, salt and pepper. Brush or drizzle evenly over the onions (picture 2), then cover with foil and bake for 45 minutes until the onions are almost tender.

Three Fry the reserved finely chopped onion in the remaining oil with the celery for about 5 minutes until softened. Add the garlic and cranberries and cook gently for 6–8 minutes until the cranberries start to soften; remove from the heat and stir in the chestnuts, parsley or coriander, salt and pepper.

Four Spoon the chestnut mixture into the onion shells (picture 3) and return to the oven for 20 minutes (picture 4).

Preparation: 30 minutes
Cooking: 1 hour 5 minutes
Makes: 12

Rosemary and
Garlic Roasties

1.6 kg/3½ lb floury potatoes,
e.g. Maris Piper

4 tablespoons olive oil

2 garlic cloves, chopped

4 tablespoons fresh
rosemary, chopped

One Peel the potatoes and cut them into chunks. Pat dry with kitchen paper (picture 1). In a bowl, mix together the oil, garlic and half the rosemary, and season.

Two Spread the potatoes out in a roasting tin and drizzle over the rosemary and garlic oil. Stir around to thoroughly coat the potatoes (picture 2); sprinkle the rest of the rosemary over the top. Cook on the shelf above the turkey for 1–1½ hours until crisp and golden.

Preparation: 10 minutes
Cooking: 1–1½ hours
Serves: 12

Sausagemeat and
Thyme Koftas

2 tablespoons olive oil

1 small onion, finely

chopped

450 g/1 lb good quality

sausagemeat

grated rind of 1 lemon

100 g/4 oz fresh white

breadcrumbs

2 teaspoons chopped fresh

thyme or 1 teaspoon dried,

plus extra sprigs

1 egg, beaten

12 rashers rindless thin-cut

streaky bacon

12 wooden or metal skewers

One Heat the olive oil in a small pan, then add the onion and fry gently for about 5 minutes, until softened and lightly browned. Remove from the heat and cool. In a bowl, mix together the meat, lemon rind, breadcrumbs and thyme (picture 1). Add the onion and oil, then add the egg and mix well, squeezing the mixture between your hands until everything is evenly mixed.

Two Divide into 12 equal pieces – they should weigh about 140 g/ 5 oz each. Press each portion around a skewer to make a sausage shape. Wrap a bacon rasher loosely around each kofta, tucking a thyme sprig between the folds (picture 2).

Three Put in a roasting tin or other shallow oven-proof dish (picture 3), and roast for 35 minutes, turning after 20 minutes.

✱ PREPARING AHEAD: These koftas can be made the day before and kept in the fridge wrapped in foil. Alternatively, wrap closely in freezer foil and freeze for up to a month.

Preparation:	45 minutes
Cooking:	35 minutes
Makes:	12

Honey Mustard
Parsnips

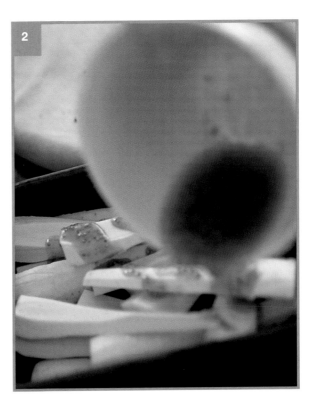

6–8 parsnips, peeled and
quartered lengthways

2 tablespoons olive oil

2 tablespoons mustard
seeds, brown or white

2 tablespoons clear honey

One Cut any woody parts from the centre of the parsnips and discard. In a bowl whisk together the oil, mustard seeds, honey, salt and pepper (picture 1).

Two Put the parsnips in a roasting tin, drizzle over the flavoured oil and toss together until they are evenly coated (picture 2). Cook for 40–50 minutes until golden.

✱ PREPARING AHEAD: Prepare the parsnips and store in a polythene bag in the fridge for up to a day.

Preparation: 10 minutes
Cooking: 40–50 minutes
Serves: 12

Port and Orange
Gravy

175 ml/6 fl oz turkey pan
juices

2 tablespoons plain flour

850 ml/1½ pints turkey stock
(see page 85)

300 ml/½ pint port

grated rind and juice of 1
orange

1 tablespoon prepared
mustard

One Heat the pan juices in the roasting tin, stir in the flour and cook for 2 minutes. Stir in the stock and port and simmer for 5 minutes (picture 1).

Two Stir in the orange rind and juice and plenty of seasoning. Bring to the boil, stirring, then stir in the mustard (picture 2). Simmer for a further 5 minutes, uncovered, until slightly thickened and glossy.

Preparation: 5 minutes
Cooking: 15 minutes
Serves: 10–12

Bread
Sauce

600 ml/1 pint full fat milk

50 g/2 oz butter

1 onion, finely chopped

6 whole cloves

2 garlic cloves

1 bay leaf

3 fresh thyme sprigs

100 g/4 oz fresh white

  breadcrumbs

4–5 tablespoons single

  cream (optional but lovely)

In a pan, simmer the milk, butter, onion, cloves, garlic and herbs for 20 minutes (picture 1). Strain (picture 2); return the milk to the pan. Add the breadcrumbs (picture 3) and simmer for 3–4 minutes. Season well with salt and pepper, then stir in the cream (picture 4), if using. Serve warm.

✱ PREPARING AHEAD: The components for this sauce can all be prepared ahead ready for the final assembly. Make and freeze the breadcrumbs up to 3 months ahead. Earlier in the day infuse the milk and strain it.

Preparation: 5 minutes
Cooking: 35 minutes
Serves: 12

All You ever Wanted to Know about Turkey

The arrival of that bird prompts a hundred questions – all of which are answered here.

WHAT SIZE TURKEY?
Allow 350–450 g/12 oz–1 lb per serving for birds up to 4.5 kg/10 lb; 200–350 g/8–12 oz for birds over 4.5 kg/10 lb (allows for leftovers).

HOW LONG WILL IT KEEP?
Supermarket fresh turkeys have a use-by date. If you buy yours from the butcher, ask how long it will keep – in general, cook within 3 days. Store loosely wrapped in a dish that will catch any drips, at the bottom of the fridge, or covered in a cold place.

FROZEN OR FRESH?
Frozen turkeys can be stored in the freezer for up to 6 months. They are much cheaper than fresh, and some are even self-basting – the turkeys are injected with sunflower oil or butter, which seeps into the meat during cooking for optimum succulence. However, they do need to be thawed carefully (see chart on page 93). A fresh bird will inevitably have a finer flavour than a frozen one.

HOW TO BUY THE BEST TURKEY
Whether buying fresh or frozen, look for a bird with a good plump breast as a scrawny bird will not be as tender. In any case, most people prefer breast meat to leg – even though the latter has a richer flavour.

When buying frozen, check that the packaging is intact and ensure that the bird is completely frozen and hasn't started to thaw.

Remember a turkey is only as good as its feed. It's worth paying extra for a corn-fed bird as its meat will have superior flavour and texture.

Don't be taken in by appearances. A smooth, white skin is not always an indication of quality. In fact, free-range birds have tougher feathers which often leave stubs in the skin. These may not look very pretty, but don't bother trying to remove them. They don't do any harm, and their presence suggests a succulent bird with flavoursome skin.

If ordering your turkey from a local butcher, ask him whether he or his suppliers hang their turkeys. Proper hanging improves the flavour and tenderness of the meat.

If you want a free-range or gourmet turkey, don't be fooled by fancy labels that may not mean anything at all. Labels such as 'farm reared' or 'farm fresh' don't have any legal definition. Instead, look out for turkeys carrying a Golden Promise label at your local butcher -these are produced by members of the Traditional Farmfresh Turkey Association, which has stringent rules governing the quality of the birds its members raise. Free-range or otherwise, the turkeys are slow-growing breeds, which develop most flavour and are properly hung.

DEFROSTING A FROZEN BIRD
Thaw your turkey on a tray, in its packaging, in a cool place such as a larder or garage. When completely thawed (check for ice crystals in the cavity) remove the packaging, giblets and neck, wipe with kitchen paper and store, loosely covered with plastic film or greaseproof paper, in the fridge at a temperature of no more than 5°C.

HOW LONG TO COOK IT FOR
As a guide, allow 20 minutes per 450 g/1 lb, plus an extra 20 minutes cooking. Above 6.75 kg/15 lb, allow 15 minutes per 450 g/1 lb, plus 15 minutes. If stuffing the turkey, reweigh after stuffing to calculate times. If your scales can't cope, bring the bathroom scales into the kitchen, get someone to stand on them, hand them the turkey and note the difference. Cover the turkey loosely with foil and cook at 180°C/Gas 4; fan oven: cook from cold at 160°C.

COOKING AND THAWING TIMES

WEIGHT OF THE BIRD	THAWING	COOKING TIME
1.3–2.25 kg/3–5 lb	20 hours	1 hour 20 minutes–2 hours
2.7–3.3 kg/6–7 lb	22 hours	2 hours 20 minutes–2 hours 40 minutes
3.6–4 kg/8–9 lb	24+ hours	3 hours–3 hours 20 minutes
4.5–5 kg/10–11 lb	24+ hours	3 hours 40 minutes–4 hours
5.5–6 kg/12–13 lb	25+ hours	5–6 hours
6.4–7 kg/14–17 lb	30+ hours	5–6 hours
8.2–9 kg/18–20 lb	45+ hours	6 hours 20 mins–7 hours

Nowadays turkeys tend to be cooked for shorter times than was once recommended. Many top chefs opt for shorter times still; but I can't recommend doing this at home as the turkey may not be fully cooked. The times given above should make sure your bird is cooked through without it being overdone or dry.

STUFFING TURKEY

Stuff the neck end only, never the body cavity, as the temperature in the centre of the bird may not rise high enough to destroy any food poisoning bacteria. The safest way to cook stuffing is in a separate dish.

THE SECRET OF A REALLY TASTY TURKEY

If you're not cooking the recipe on page 84, where the bird is basted with butter, then it's a good idea to roast your turkey upside-down on its breast; this enables the juices from the back and legs to run down to the breast, keeping it moist. To prevent the flesh drying out, baste the bird with butter or olive oil, cover loosely with a sheet of foil and baste every 30–40 minutes. Remove the foil for the last 40 minutes of cooking time to crisp the skin.

Cook a smaller bird in a large roasting bag. Remove from bag for the last 30 minutes and baste.

To check that your turkey is fully cooked, pierce the thickest part of the thigh with a skewer. Leave for a minute – initial juices may be clouded with fat, then the juices should run clear. If you have a meat thermometer, check that the centre of the bird has reached 75°C/167°F to ensure any salmonella is destroyed.

When the turkey is cooked, remove from the oven, cover with either foil or a clean cloth and leave to rest (see timeplan, page 83). This makes carving easier and the turkey will become more succulent; it also gives you time to make the gravy.

HOW TO MAKE WONDERFUL TURKEY GRAVY

Again, if you're not cooking my Port and Orange Gravy, this makes the more traditional version. First make giblet stock: rinse the giblets and put in a pan with 600 ml/1 pint cold water, half an onion, a carrot and a celery stick, a few black peppercorns, 2 bay leaves and a few parsley and/or thyme sprigs. Bring to the boil, then reduce the heat and simmer, partly covered, for 1 hour. Strain and cool. When cold, chill for up to 1 day before use, or freeze.

To make the gravy, put the bird on a carving plate and cover. Pour off the fat from the roasting tin, leaving just the meat juices and 1 tablespoon of fat, then set the tin on the hob over a medium heat and stir in 1 tablespoon of plain flour. Cook for 1 minute, stirring and scraping up any bits from the bottom of the tin with a wire whisk. Gradually stir in the stock, then add a splash of wine if you wish and season with salt and pepper. Pour any juices from the turkey into the gravy. Let it simmer while the turkey rests and is carved, by which time the gravy will be ready to serve.

SAVING THE LEFTOVERS

Cool leftover turkey quickly by putting it on a cold plate and letting it stand in a cool place. When cold, wrap well in foil or plastic film, then store in the fridge for up to 3 days. Meat removed from the bone may also be frozen, packed in freezer bags or boxes, for up to 2 months. Meat frozen in gravy will be moister.

Mince Pies

Gluten-free flour makes crumbly pastry, so for best results roll it out between sheets of non-stick baking parchment or plastic film. Store and freeze like normal mince pies.

280 g/10 oz gluten-free flour

140 g/5 oz butter, plus extra

2 tablespoons caster sugar

250 g/9 oz gluten-free
  mincemeat

a little milk, for glazing

3 tablespoons flaked
  almonds

Preparation: 25 minutes, plus 5 minutes cooling

Cooking: 15 minutes

Makes: 12

One Preheat the oven to 200°C/Gas 6/fan oven 180°C. Lightly grease a 12-hole bun tin with butter. Sift the flour into a bowl, then rub in the butter until the mixture resembles coarse breadcrumbs. Stir in half the sugar, then add about 2 tablespoons of water and mix to a soft but not sticky dough. (If it's too soft to handle, wrap and chill for 30 minutes.)

Two Roll out the pastry and cut out 12 pie bases using a 7 cm/2³/₄ in plain or fluted cutter. Transfer these rounds to the bun tin and fill with heaped teaspoonfuls of mincemeat. Cut 12 slightly smaller rounds (about 6 cm/¹/₂ in) for lids. Moisten the edge of each base with water and affix the lids, pressing the edges to seal. Brush the tops with a little milk and scatter over a few almonds. Sprinkle with the remaining sugar and bake for 15 minutes. Cool the mince pies in the tin for 5 minutes before removing, as they crumble if removed while still warm.

CHRISTMAS ON A SPECIAL DIET

Christmas Pudding

140 g/5 oz fresh gluten-free
   bread

100 g/4 oz butter, melted,
   plus extra

50 g/2 oz rice flour

½ teaspoon ground cinnamon

1 teaspoon mixed spice

½ teaspoon gluten-free
   baking powder

100 g/4 oz cooking apple,
   peeled and grated

400 g/4 oz carrot, grated

400 g/14 oz mixed dried fruit

100 g/4 oz light muscovado
   sugar

50 g/2 oz chopped mixed peel

50 g/2 oz ground almonds

1 tablespoon black treacle

2 eggs, beaten

finely grated rind of ½ lemon
   and ½ orange

2 tablespoons sherry
   (optional)

Preparation: 25 minutes

Cooking: 4 hours, plus 2 hours
reheating on day of serving

Serves: 8

One Break the bread into pieces and whizz to fine crumbs in a food processor; set aside. Grease and line the base of a 1.2–1.4 litre/ 2–2½ pint pudding basin with greaseproof paper. Sift together the rice flour, spices and baking powder. Add the melted butter, apple, carrot, dried fruit, breadcrumbs, sugar, peel and almonds. Mix thoroughly.

Two Heat the treacle until just warm. Remove from the heat and stir in the eggs, citrus rind and sherry, if using. Mix into the flour and fruit, then spoon the mixture into the prepared basin. Cover with a double thickness of greaseproof paper, tie to secure and overlap foil. Put into a large pan and pour in boiling water to come one-third of the way up the basin. Bring to the boil, then cover and steam for 4 hours, until the pud is risen and firm to the touch. Cool completely, then top with greaseproof paper, wrap in foil and keep in a cool dry place. To reheat, steam for 2 hours.

Seasonal Entertaining

CHRISTMAS IS SUCH a sociable time and many of us will be planning to catch up with old friends over a cosy candlelit meal, invite the neighbours in for drinks or perhaps host a big, noisy, family get-together. In theory this is wonderful, but set amongst the other feverish activities, such as shopping, present wrapping and cooking everyday food for the family, it can be a daunting prospect.

The following pages are packed with recipes that look glamorous without being fussy, taste superb with minimum effort, and can be made ahead or in convenient stages so that you can fit the cooking around all the other calls on your time and energy. There are three seasonal starters to choose from, and four alternative roasts, including step-by-step instructions for roasting a perfect goose with all the trimmings. If you have vegetarians to cater for we have two dishes that will make them feel very spoilt, and the four luscious puddings include two that you can tuck away in the freezer several weeks ahead. Those who are not fans of traditional Christmas fruit cakes but like to have something to offer guests at teatime can choose from a rich buttery stollen or an Italian panforte which is just bursting with nuts, spices and honey. If you love mixing cocktails or making mulled wine when friends drop by, Sarah Jane Evans has a clutch of recipes to choose from, though I have to confess my favourite is the Swedish Glögg, which smells and tastes of all that is good about Christmas. And when the last guest has left and you find all sorts of bits and pieces lurking in the fridge, turn to our chapter on leftovers for some fresh, inspiring dishes all the family will love.

Whatever dishes you choose to make, the following recipes will make sure that you enjoy hassle-free entertaining, and you can be sure they will turn out well for you, as every recipe is thoroughly tested in the Good Food kitchen. Step-by-step instructions guide you and ensure success every time, and as the freezer is your most important kitchen ally at this time of year, preparing ahead, storing, and freezing instructions are given for each recipe.

On the menu

FESTIVE STARTERS

- PLATTER OF ARBROATH SMOKIES
- POTTED HAM WITH BEETROOT AND RED ONION SALAD
- CELERIAC AND PARSLEY SOUP WITH CRUMBLED STILTON

ALTERNATIVE ROASTS

- ROAST GOOSE
- GLAZED TURKEY CROWN
- BEEF WELLINGTON
- SALMON AND WATERCRESS PUFF

VEGETARIAN OPTIONS

- MANJU MALHI'S MASALA NUT ROAST
- MIXED MUSHROOM AND CHESTNUT PIES

FESTIVE PUDS

- FROZEN DAIRY-FREE CHRISTMAS PUDDING
- ICED RASPBERRY CRANACHAN TRIFLE
- BRIAN GLOVER'S VANILLA AND CLEMENTINE ICE CREAM TERRINE
- CHOCOLATE CHRISTMAS PUDDING

FESTIVE CAKES

- STOLLEN
- BRIAN GLOVER'S WHITE IVY CAKE
- PANFORTE

LEFTOVERS

- BOXING DAY SOUP
- SHERRIED TURKEY AND HAM BAKE
- WINTER CRUNCH SALAD
- SILVANA FRANCO'S CHRISTMAS PUDDING ICE CREAM

DRINKS

- MIX IT!
- GLÖGG

Platter of
Arbroath Smokies

3 pairs Arbroath smokies

2 large cucumbers

1 small onion, thinly sliced
   into wedges

50 g/2 oz golden caster
   sugar

6 tablespoons white wine
   vinegar

2 tablespoons mustard
   seeds (optional)

4 tablespoons creamed
   horseradish sauce

500ml/17 fl oz tub crème
   fraîche

1 large bunch parsley,
   chopped

4 large lemons

warm soda bread, to serve

**Preparation: 2¼ hours,
including soaking and chilling**
Serves: 8

One Open the smokies and
remove the flesh in large pieces,
discarding the skin and bone. Put
on a large platter, cover with cling
film and keep in the fridge.

Two Thinly slice the cucumbers
without peeling, then layer the
slices with the onion in a colander,
sprinkling with a little salt. Set
aside for about 1 hour. Rinse
under cold running water to
remove excess salt. Pat the
cucumber and onion dry on
kitchen paper.

Three Put the sugar in a large
bowl and stir in 4 tablespoons of
boiling water. When the sugar has
dissolved, add the vinegar and the
cucumber mixture. Season with
pepper, stir in the mustard seeds
(if using). Cover and chill for 1 hour
or overnight.

Four Remove the platter from the
fridge and allow to come to room
temperature. Mix the horseradish
and crème fraîche. Stir the parsley
into the cucumber pickle. Cut the
lemons into wedges and arrange
on the platter. Serve with the
cucumber pickle, horseradish
cream and warm bread.

✱ PREPARING AHEAD:
Prepare the smokie platter and
cucumber pickle up to the end
of step three and chill overnight.
Finish the dish from step four
on the day.

✱ ALTERNATIVE TO SMOKIES:
If you are unable to get Arbroath
smokies, use skinless smoked
trout fillets instead, although they
will give different flavour. You will
find them in the chiller cabinet
of large supermarkets alongside
the fresh prawns.

Potted Ham
with Beetroot and Red Onion Salad

FOR THE HAM

900 g/2 lb piece unsmoked shoulder of ham

2 bay leaves

1 onion, cut into wedges

1 teaspoon black peppercorns

2 celery sticks, chopped

100 g/4 oz butter

good pinch each allspice and mace

   or nutmeg

FOR THE SALAD

200 g/8 oz cooked beetroot

1 red onion

8 cornichons or small gherkins

2 teaspoons small capers, drained of their

   vinegar or rinsed of salt

FOR THE DRESSING

1 teaspoon wholegrain mustard

1 tablespoon sherry vinegar

   or red wine vinegar

3 tablespoons olive oil

winter salad leaves, such as lamb's lettuce,

   endive and radicchio

wholemeal toast or soda bread,

   to serve

This recipe is easily doubled, and the potted ham can be made in one large bowl if you are serving it buffet style.

One Put the ham in a pan with cold water to cover. Add the bay leaves, onion wedges, peppercorns and celery to the water. Bring to the boil, then skim off the scum and simmer for 1 hour until the ham is very tender. Leave to cool in the water.

Two Lift out the ham, trim off excess fat and skin, then shred the meat with two forks or finely chop with a sharp knife and transfer to a bowl. Measure 300ml/$\frac{1}{2}$ pint of the cooking liquid and mix into the ham.

Three Melt the butter in a small pan. When it comes to the boil, skim off the foam that settles on the top with a tablespoon. Carefully pour the clarified butter into a clean bowl, leaving the milky residue in the bottom of the pan. Stir the spices into the clarified butter.

Four Pack the ham into six 150ml/$\frac{1}{4}$ pint ramekin dishes, then pour the clarified butter over the top. Cool, then chill until set (about 2 hours, or overnight if more convenient).

Five Finely chop the beetroot and onion. Slice the cornichons and add to the beetroot with the capers, mixing well. Whisk together the mustard, vinegar, oil, and season to taste with salt and freshly ground black pepper, then pour half over the beetroot salad. Cover and chill for up to 4 hours.

Six To serve, set the ramekins on side plates. Pile a handful of winter salad leaves on each plate and spoon the beetroot salad on top. Drizzle over the remaining dressing and serve with whole-meal toast or soda bread.

✱ PREPARING AHEAD: The potted hams can be cooked up to 3 days ahead. Chill until set, then store in the fridge until ready to serve. The beetroot and red onion salad and dressing can be prepared 4 hours ahead.

Preparation: 45–55 minutes, plus 4 hours chilling

Cooking: 1 hour

Serves: 6

Celeriac and Parsley Soup
with Crumbled Stilton

Celeriac has all of the flavour of celery without the stringiness, and it purées down to a velvety smoothness. Walnut bread is the perfect accompaniment.

25 g/1 oz butter

1 tablespoon vegetable oil

2 large or 3 medium onions, chopped

1 large carrot, chopped

700 g/1 lb 9 oz celeriac

1.4 litres/2½ pints vegetable stock

few sprigs fresh thyme

300 ml/½ pint milk

15–20 g pack fresh curly parsley

140–175 g/5–6 oz Stilton

walnut bread, to serve

Preparation: 20–30 minutes
Cooking: 35–40 minutes
Serves: 6–8

One Melt the butter and oil in
a large pan, add the onions and
carrot and fry gently for 6 minutes,
until the onion is softened.
Meanwhile, peel the celeriac and
cut into 2.5 cm/1 in chunks.

Two Add the celeriac to the pan,
stir well, then add the stock
and thyme. Bring to the boil,
stir, then cover and simmer for
20–25 minutes, until the vegetables
are tender.

Three Purée the soup in a blender.
You will need to do this in batches,
so have a heatproof bowl handy.
Return it to the pan, stir in the milk
and season. Chop the parsley and
stir into the soup. Crumble the
Stilton and sprinkle over each
portion before serving with slices
of walnut bread.

✱ PREPARING AHEAD:
You can make the soup the day
before. Chill and gently reheat
in a saucepan for 5 minutes.
Alternatively chill, then freeze the
soup up to 3 months in advance.
Defrost the soup in the microwave or tip the frozen or chilled
soup into a large pan and gently
reheat, then simmer for 5 minutes.
Stir in the parsley and sprinkle
the Stilton over the hot soup.

Roast
Goose

Jeni Wright's rich and
succulent roast goose is
a spectacular alternative
to turkey. The sweet and
spicy stuffing is full of
Middle Eastern flavours.
Apples and shallots are
roasted as accompani-
ments, and orange juice
and port are stirred into
the meat juices in this
gravy that is sweetened
with redcurrant jelly.

✱ PREPARING AHEAD: Make
the giblet stock and the stuffing
the day before roasting the
goose. Cool, then keep them in
covered containers in the fridge.

Preparation: 45–60 minutes
Cooking: 3 hours, plus 30
minutes resting
Serves: 6–8

FOR THE GOOSE

**4.5 kg/10 lb trussed
and oven-ready fresh
goose, with giblets**
sea or rock salt
**fresh mint, parsley and
bay leaves, to garnish**

FOR THE STOCK

**giblets from the goose
(excluding fat and liver)**
½ large onion, sliced
pared rind of 1 large orange
**a small handful of parsley
stalks**
2 bay leaves, torn
about 6 black peppercorns

FOR THE STUFFING

2 tablespoons olive oil
½ large onion, finely chopped
**2 celery sticks, finely
chopped**
1 teaspoon ground coriander
250 g/9 oz lean minced pork
**140 g/5 oz fresh granary or
wholemeal breadcrumbs**
**85 g/3 oz ready-to-eat dried
apricots, finely chopped**
**finely grated rind of 1 large
orange**
**3 tablespoons chopped
fresh parsley**
**2 tablespoons chopped
fresh mint**

FOR THE GRAVY

2 tablespoons plain flour

600 ml/1 pint giblet stock

juice of 1 orange

4–6 tablespoons port, to taste

1 tablespoon redcurrant jelly

MAKE THE STOCK

One Put the giblets in a pan with 1.7 litres/3 pints cold water. Bring to the boil and skim off the scum. Add the onion slices, orange rind, parsley stalks, bay leaves and peppercorns. Simmer for 1½–2 hours, with the pan lid tilted, until reduced by two-thirds.

Two Strain the stock into a measuring jug – you will need about 600ml/1 pint. Cover and leave to cool. Chill until needed.

MAKE THE STUFFING

One Heat the oil in a frying pan, add the onion, celery and coriander and fry gently, stirring, for 10 minutes until softened but not browned. Transfer to a large bowl and leave to cool.

Two Add the remaining stuffing ingredients, plus 1 teaspoon of salt and plenty of pepper. Use your hands to mix well, squeezing the mixture so that the ingredients bind together evenly.

COOK THE GOOSE

One Preheat the oven to 190°C/Gas 5/fan oven 170°C. Make sure you have removed the giblets and then wipe inside the body cavity with kitchen paper,

before spooning the stuffing mixture inside. You can easily do this with the legs still tied. Put the goose in a large roasting tin that will hold it comfortably. Prick the breast gently with a fork all over and sprinkle with sea or rock salt (picture 1).

Two Cut two sheets of heavy-duty foil, about 100 × 50cm/40 × 20in each. Put lengthways and over-lapping by an inch or so on a work surface (the kitchen table is ideal). Put the tin in the centre; bring the foil up around the tin and goose to enclose them (picture 2). Scrunch the edges of the foil to make a loose tent over the goose. Roast on the second shelf from the bottom of the oven for 1½ hours.

Three After the goose has been roasting for 1½ hours, remove from the oven and open the foil. Using a baster, ladle or large spoon, baste the goose (picture 3), then remove as much fat as possible from the tin and reserve it. Cover the goose again and roast for 1 hour. Remove from the oven and open up the foil to expose the breast (keep the foil on the legs as they need extra protection). Baste, remove and reserve the fat as before. Return to the oven with the breast exposed; roast for 30 minutes to brown the skin.

Four To test if the goose is cooked, pierce the thickest part of the thigh with a skewer (picture 4) – the juices should run clear, not pink or red. Carefully lift the goose out of the foil and tin and hold it with the legs facing downwards to drain off as much excess fat as possible. Put the goose on a large warmed platter. Cover it loosely with fresh foil

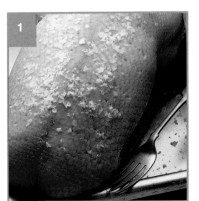

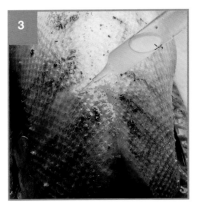

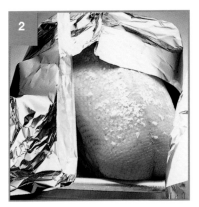

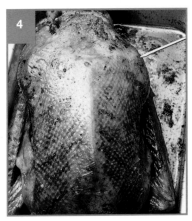

and leave to rest in a warm place for 30 minutes – this is important as during this time the meat fibres relax and the juices settle, making carving the meat easier.

Five Pour off all but about 1 tablespoon of fat from the tin (use some for roasting the potatoes). Put the tin on top of the stove over a low heat. Sprinkle in the flour and stir with a wooden spoon to scrape up the sediment until the flour is well browned. Pour in a little stock and stir to mix in (picture 5). Increase the heat and continue adding stock in this way. When it has come to the boil, simmer, stirring, for 5 minutes. Add the redcurrant jelly, port and orange juice and simmer, stirring, until the jelly melts and the gravy thickens.

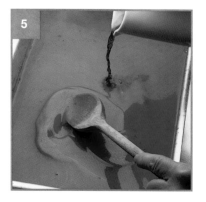

Six Garnish the goose with herbs, roast apples, shallots and stuffing balls if you like (see recipes on this page) before transferring to a carving board. Cut the breasts away from the rib cage (this is easier if you remove the wishbone) and carve them diagonally into slices. Cut off the legs, then shave off the meat by holding each leg by the knuckle and slicing down towards the board. Cut off the wings and fillets (the oyster meat where the legs meet the body on the underside). Use a long-handled spoon to remove the stuffing.

ACCOMPANIMENTS FOR GOOSE

✱ STUFFING BALLS

These can be served around the bird. Make double the quantity of stuffing and put half in the bird and shape half into 24 balls. Fry these for a few minutes in hot olive oil or goose fat until golden brown all over. Drain on kitchen paper, then put in a baking dish and bake for about 30 minutes on the shelf above the goose. If you are short of oven space, you can add them to the tin of roasting potatoes.

✱ ROAST POTATOES

Potatoes roasted in goose fat are golden, crisp and delicious – the best roast potatoes ever. For 6–8 people, peel 1.8 kg/4 lb potatoes and halve or quarter them depending on their size. Parboil them in salted water for 10 minutes. Drain and return the potatoes to the pan, then toss over a low heat to dry them out and rough up the surface (this makes them extra crisp). Put 4 tablespoons of the liquid fat

collected from the goose into a large roasting tin. Heat in the oven on the shelf above the goose until very hot, then add the potatoes in a single layer. Roast the potatoes for 1 hour, turning them over halfway through. Sprinkle with sea or rock salt.

✱ ROASTED APPLES AND SHALLOTS

Score around the circumferences of small, red-skinned apples and put in a tin. Drizzle with a little oil, then roast with the goose for 25 minutes (picture 6) – no longer or they'll collapse. Keep shallots in their skins, cut them in half lengthways, drizzle with oil, sprinkle with salt and pepper, and roast for 25–30 minutes (picture 7).

OTHER ALTERNATIVES

Sharp fruity sauces and jellies, such as gooseberry, apple, redcurrant, lingonberry and cranberry, also complement goose. Braised red cabbage, Brussels sprouts with chestnuts and a purée of parsnip, carrot, swede or celeriac also make very good accompaniments.

All You ever Wanted to Know about Goose

COOKING TIMES

Geese weighing 4.5–6.3 kg/10–14 lb have been specially bred to have a high meat-to-bone ratio and are a good size for Christmas lunch.

We cooked a 4.5 kg/10 lb bird for our recipe. If your goose is not the same weight you will need to adjust the cooking time using this formula – allow 15 minutes per 450 g/1 lb, plus an extra 30 minutes. If you are stuffing the goose, weigh it after stuffing, then calculate the cooking time. We suggest the following timings: a 4.5 kg/10 lb bird will take 3 hours to roast and will serve 6–8 people; a 5.4 kg/12 lb goose will take 3½ hours to roast and will serve 8–10 people; a 6.3 kg/14 lb goose will take 4 hours to roast and will serve 10–12 people.

On the day of roasting, calculate your timings backwards from the time you plan to serve the meal, remembering to allow time for preheating the oven at the beginning and resting time for the goose at the end.

For more information and recipes contact The Goose Information Bureau. Its helpline is open 8am–5.30pm Monday to Friday; call 01603 616 097.

WHERE TO GET YOUR GOOSE

Geese are only available for a limited season. Traditionally the first goose is eaten at Michaelmas (29 September) so from this time on you will be able to buy them, but only up to Christmas and the New Year. This makes goose a real treat for the festive period.

For a fresh free-range goose for Christmas or the New Year, consult your butcher. For collection on 23 or 24 December, he will probably need your order by the end of the first week in December at the latest.

WHICH GOOSE?

For the very best results, buy a free-range, traditionally reared goose. The meat will be tender and tasty, the skin crisp. Avoid a bird that looks dark and shallow breasted, or one which has a prominent breast-bone and scrawny legs. These will not have much meat and may be tough.

HOW TO STORE

If cooking for Christmas, collect the goose on the 23 or 24 December. As soon as you get the bird home, take it out of its bag or box. Oven-ready birds have their wings trussed with string to keep them close to the body. The legs and parson's nose are also tied together with string. Don't untie any of these strings or the goose will not keep its shape during roasting. Put the goose on a tray, cover it loosely with foil and store it in the fridge or a cold larder. If you don't have room in the fridge, store it in an unheated room, shed or garage.

FREEZING A GOOSE

If you are planning to cook the goose after Christmas Day or Boxing Day (say for New Year's Eve), you will need to freeze it if you have collected it on the 23 or 24 December. Freeze it, with giblets inside, immediately you get home after collecting it. This short freezing time will do it no harm, but remember to allow at least 24 hours thawing time in the fridge or in a cold place such as the garage before stuffing and roasting.

COOKING WITH THE GIBLETS

Remove the giblets. They will be in a plastic bag, either inside the bird or packed separately. The bag will contain the neck and gizzard (these are the actual giblets), the liver and some white fat. If you are not making the giblet stock immediately, put the giblets in a bowl, cover and keep in the fridge for up to 24 hours. The liver can be chopped and used in the stuffing for the goose if you like, or it can be fried in goose fat and eaten on its own, or used to make pâté. The white fat can be rendered down, then cooled and chilled for use as a cooking fat.

COOKING WITH GOOSE FAT

Goose fat is both monounsaturated and polyunsaturated, so it resembles olive oil in its chemical composition. This means it is actually good for you. Plus, it tastes great, so don't discard it.

Render down the white fat that comes with the goose by melting it gently in a pan. Strain it through muslin into a glass or china bowl or jam jar. It will keep in the fridge or freezer for up to 6 months.

Rendered white fat can be used for frying and roasting, and for sealing cooked pâtés and terrines. It also makes excellent rich pastry – grate it while frozen, otherwise it is too soft to handle well.

The liquid fat from cooking can be used for roasting potatoes, but you only need a little. Chilled, it will keep for 3 weeks. Use for roasting vegetables, meat, poultry and game. Strain the excess fat as above.

Glazed
Turkey Crown

This cut feeds up to 6 people, and it's easy to carve into the bargain. What's more, if you prefer white meat, that's all you'll get. Most supermarkets now sell turkey crowns as well as whole turkeys, and some even come ready stuffed. In this recipe, the glaze has a slightly sweet oriental flavour and gives the turkey added glamour for little extra effort.

FOR THE TURKEY

2 kg/4 lb 8oz turkey
   breast joint (with or
   without stuffing)
1 clementine, thinly sliced
340 g/12 oz pack cocktail
   sausages
2 teaspoons cornflour
300 ml/½ pint chicken
   or vegetable stock
2 tablespoons sherry
bay leaves, to garnish

FOR THE MARINADED
WRAPS

2 tablespoons teriyaki
   marinade
1 tablespoon clear honey
juice of 1 clementine
3 leeks, trimmed and
   washed (see tip)
16 rashers rindless
   streaky bacon

MAKE THE MARINADED WRAPS

One Mix the teriyaki marinade, honey and clementine juice.

Two Cut the leeks into 5 cm/2 in pieces and wrap a rasher of bacon around each one, securing with cocktail sticks (picture 1). Toss them in some of the marinade.

COOK THE TURKEY

One Preheat the oven to 190°C/Gas 5/fan oven 170°C. Weigh the turkey with the stuffing and calculate the cooking time at 18 minutes per 450 g/1 lb. Put the turkey in a large roasting tin.

Two Roast the turkey for 50 minutes, brush with marinade, arrange the clementine slices over the breast and brush again (picture 2). Put the bacon-wrapped leeks around the turkey, along with the sausages and roast for the remaining time, occasionally basting with the pan juices.

Three Transfer to a warm serving platter, garnish with bay leaves and cover with foil. Leave to rest for 20 minutes.

Four Blend the cornflour with a little cold water. Add to the roasting tin along with the stock and sherry. Bring to the boil and stir until slightly thickened. Serve with the turkey.

Preparation:	20 minutes
Cooking:	1 hour 20 minutes, plus 20 minutes resting time
Serves:	4–6, with plenty of leftovers

✱ PREPARING AHEAD: The bacon-wrapped leeks and the teriyaki sauce can be made a day ahead and chilled separately. Toss the wraps in the teriyaki sauce when ready to cook.

✱ WASHING YOUR GREENS: Clean the leeks thoroughly by slitting them down the length to the centre, then opening out the layers and washing under cold running water. Drain well and cut into 5 cm/2 in pieces.

Beef
Wellington

This is definitely for a special occasion, as the whole fillet is an expensive cut. But it looks spectacular and tastes and cuts like a dream. Sunblush or sun-dried tomatoes give the stuffing a sweet, tangy note that provides a good balance with the rich meat.

1.3 kg/3 lb fillet of beef from the thick end

1 tablespoon olive oil

25 g/1 oz butter

1 red onion, finely chopped

300 g/10 oz chestnut mushrooms, chopped

2 tablespoons sherry

2 teaspoons fresh oregano, or 1 teaspoon dried

100 g/4 oz Sunblush or sun-dried tomatoes

500 g/1 lb pack puff pastry, thawed if frozen

beaten egg, to glaze

rocket leaves, to garnish

FOR THE GRAVY

1 tablespoon plain flour

425 ml/¾ pint beef stock

300 ml/½ pint red wine

2 teaspoons wholegrain mustard

Preparation:	30–45 minutes
Cooking:	1 hour 10 minutes–1 hour 35 minutes
Serves:	6–8

One Preheat the oven to 200°C/Gas 6/fan oven 180°C. Tie the meat with string at 2.5cm/1in intervals along the length of the joint to keep it in shape. Heat the oil in a large frying pan, add the beef and fry on a high heat for 5–8 minutes, turning occasionally, until evenly browned. Transfer to a roasting tin and roast for 20 minutes for rare, 25–30 minutes for medium rare and 35–40 minutes for medium to well done. Timings will depend on the thickness of the joint, so use your judgement. If, when you press the joint with your finger, it feels very bouncy it will be rare, if slightly firmer it will be medium, if firm, it will be well done. Remove from the oven and leave to cool. Transfer to a plate and reserve the tin juices. Snip off string and season all over.

Two To make the stuffing, add the butter to the pan in which the beef was fried. When foaming, add the onion. Fry for 5 minutes until softened. Add the mushrooms, fry at a moderate heat until softened, about 5 minutes. Add the sherry, salt and pepper. Fry until no juices remain. Remove from heat, stir in the oregano and tomatoes and leave to cool.

Three Roll out the pastry on a lightly floured surface until it is large enough to wrap around and completely enclose the meat (reserve any juices that have come from the meat). It should be 8 cm/3 1/4 in longer at each end and 15 cm/6 in wider on each side than the meat. Trim off any excess pastry.

Four Arrange half the stuffing down the central third of the pastry. Sit the beef on top (picture 1). Put the remaining stuffing on top.

Five Brush the pastry edges with beaten egg. Bring the pastry over the ends of beef, brush these with egg, then bring the sides over so they overlap slightly and seal in the edges (picture 2). Invert onto a baking sheet so that the join is underneath the meat.

Six Brush the pastry well with egg. With a sharp pointed knife, mark diagonal lines to make a criss-cross pattern, taking care not to cut right through the pastry. Chill until ready to cook (at least 30 minutes to set the pastry, or up to 24 hours).

Seven Meanwhile make the gravy. Reheat the pan juices in the roasting tin, stir in the flour and cook for 1 minute. Stir in the stock and wine, scraping the pan base to release any sticky bits. Add the mustard and any reserved juices, then simmer until reduced by half, about 10 minutes. Strain through a sieve if needed. Taste and season.

Eight Preheat the oven to 200°C/Gas 6/fan oven 180°C. Cook the beef until pastry is crisp and golden, 40–45 minutes. Transfer the beef to a serving platter and leave to rest for 5 minutes. Scatter rocket leaves around the beef. Serve in thick slices with the gravy passed around separately.

✱ PREPARING AHEAD: You can assemble the Wellington up to step seven and chill overnight in the fridge. Cover and chill the gravy and reheat. Cook as in step eight.

Salmon and
Watercress Puff

1.3 kg/3 lb whole salmon, filleted

　and skinned

200 g/8 oz full fat soft cheese

bunch of fresh watercress, finely chopped

grated rind of 1 orange

500 g/1 lb packet puff pastry, thawed if frozen

beaten egg, to glaze

new potatoes, to serve

FOR THE SALAD

3 oranges, segmented

bunch of fresh watercress

½ tablespoon orange juice

1 teaspoon balsamic vinegar

1½ tablespoon olive oil

One Sprinkle the salmon fillets all over with salt and pepper. To make the filling, soften the cheese and beat in the chopped watercress and the orange rind; season. Lay one fillet, skinned-side down, and spread with the filling. Cover with other fillet, skinned-side up (picture 1).

Two Roll out half the pastry so it is 2.5cm/1in larger all round than the fish. Put on a dampened baking sheet; lay the salmon in the centre. Brush the pastry edges with egg. Roll out the remaining pastry to cover; trim off excess. Pinch edges to seal.

Three Brush the top with egg. Score a criss-cross pattern on top. Cover and chill for at least 30 minutes.

Four Preheat oven to 220°C/Gas 7/fan oven 200°C. Bake the puff for 20 minutes, then glaze again. Lower to 160°C/Gas 3/fan oven 140°C and cook for 20–25 minutes.

MAKE THE SALAD

One Mix the orange segments and watercress leaves. Whisk together the juice, vinegar and oil; season. Dress the salad.

Two Serve with the salmon puff and new potatoes.

✱ PREPARING AHEAD: You can assemble the puff to the end of step two up to 4 hours ahead. Cover and chill until ready to cook.

Preparation:	15 minutes, plus 30 minutes chilling
Cooking:	45 minutes
Serves:	6

MANJU MALHI'S

Masala
Nut Roast

As more and more people choose not to eat meat, I find it increasingly useful to have a good range of vegetarian recipes at my fingertips. Manju, despite being a Hindu, still joins in all the festivities, and her nut roast is ideal if you have vegetarians coming for Christmas lunch.

Preparation: 30 minutes

Cooking: 1¼ hours

Serves: 6

2 tablespoons vegetable oil

2 medium onions, finely chopped

1 fresh green chilli, seeded and finely
    chopped (optional)

6 garlic cloves, crushed

2 teaspoons medium or hot curry powder

2 teaspoons tomato purée

½ teaspoon salt

5 cm/2 in piece of fresh root ginger,
    grated

1 small potato, peeled and grated

2 medium carrots, peeled and grated

300 g/10 oz cauliflower florets, grated

140 g/5 oz mixed nuts, chopped
    and toasted

25 g/1 oz fresh coriander leaves, chopped,
    plus extra leaves to garnish

100 g/4 oz toasted breadcrumbs

1 egg, beaten

FOR THE TOMATO GRAVY

1 tablespoon vegetable oil

¼ teaspoon brown or black mustard seeds

1 medium onion, finely chopped

25 g/1 oz butter

1 teaspoon ground cumin

¼ teaspoon chilli powder (optional)

¼ teaspoon ground black pepper

¼ teaspoon salt

500 g/1 lb 2 oz passata (smooth thick
    sieved tomatoes) – sold in jars
    or cartons

2 teaspoons golden granulated sugar

MAKE THE NUT ROAST

One Preheat the oven to 190ºC/Gas 5/fan oven 170ºC. Grease a 1 kg/2 lb loaf tin and line with greaseproof paper.

Two Heat the oil in a saucepan and fry the onions for 5 minutes until softened. Add the chilli, garlic, curry powder, tomato purée, salt and ginger and fry for 1 minute. Tip in the potato, carrots and cauliflower and fry for 2 minutes.

Three Remove from the heat, stir in the nuts and coriander, then the breadcrumbs and the egg. Mix well, spoon into the tin and pack down tightly. Cover the tin loosely with foil and roast for 1 hour. Remove the foil and roast for a further 15 minutes. The surface of the loaf should be lightly browned.

MAKE THE TOMATO GRAVY

One Heat the oil in a saucepan and sprinkle in a few mustard seeds. Wait until they crackle and pop, then carefully add the rest. Tip in the onion and butter and fry for 5–6 minutes until soft and golden.

Two Add the cumin, chilli powder (if using), pepper and salt and stir to combine. Fry for 1–2 minutes, then pour in the passata and about 4 tablespoons water. Stir and add a little more water if too thick. Simmer for 5–10 minutes, then stir in the sugar and remove from the heat. Season to taste.

TO SERVE

Remove the roast from the oven and leave to stand in its tin for 5 minutes. Carefully turn it out onto a platter and discard the paper. Serve garnished with coriander, with the tomato gravy in a jug.

✱ MAKING TOASTED BREADCRUMBS:
To make 100 g/4 oz toasted breadcrumbs, blitz 140 g/5 oz white or brown bread in a food processor to fine crumbs. Scatter into a roasting tin and put in the oven when you turn it on to preheat for the roast. Cook for 10–12 minutes, tossing the crumbs every 3–4 minutes until they're totally dry and a golden colour.

Mixed Mushroom and Chestnut Pies

These rich puff-pastry-topped pies are easy to make and look spectacular.

25 g/1 oz butter

2 tablespoons olive oil

2 shallots, chopped

3 leeks, about 450 g/1 lb
   in trimmed weight, sliced

2 garlic cloves, finely chopped

450 g/1 lb mixed mushrooms,
   such as chestnut, button,
   girolle and shiitake, halved
   or quartered if large, and
   wiped clean

4 tablespoons sherry

200 g/7 oz vacuum pack cooked
   chestnuts

1 tablespoon fresh thyme leaves

2 tablespoons fresh parsley

200 ml/7 fl oz carton crème
   fraîche

500 g/1 lb packet puff pastry

1 beaten egg, to glaze

sprigs of fresh thyme, to garnish

One Melt the butter and 1 tablespoon of the oil in a large frying pan, then cook the shallots, leeks and garlic for 4–5 minutes until softened and starting to brown (picture 1).

Two Add the remaining tablespoon of oil and the mixed mushrooms (picture 2) and fry for 5 minutes until the juices just start to run. Over a fairly high heat, stir in the sherry and let it bubble for 1 minute. Stir in the chestnuts, thyme leaves, chopped parsley and crème fraîche (picture 3). Spoon the mixture into four round 300 ml/½ pint (13 cm/5 in) ovenproof dishes, and cool.

Three Meanwhile, preheat the oven to 220°C/Gas 7/fan oven 200°C. Roll out the pastry fairly thickly (just over 5 mm/¼ in thick), then cut out four circles slightly larger than the diameter of the dishes. Using the pastry trimmings, cut out 5 mm/¼ in wide strips of pastry. Brush the dish rims with water and stick the pastry strips round the rims. Brush the strips with water and put the lids on top (picture 4). Press to seal (picture 5) and knock up the edges with the back of a knife to seal and flake up.

Four Make a small hole in the centre of each pastry lid with the point of a knife, brush the pastry with beaten egg, and sprinkle with freshly ground black pepper. Put the pies on a baking sheet and bake for about 15 minutes until the pastry is puffed and golden. Garnish with sprigs of thyme.

✱ PREPARING AHEAD:
Make the filling the day before, cool, cover and chill. Put the pastry lids on the pies earlier in the morning and keep chilled; allow 20 minutes for the pies to cook. If you really don't want to roll out pastry on the day, you can put the pastry lids on the pies the night before, but keep them chilled.

✱ STILTON VARIATION:
For extra richness, crumble 85 g/3 oz Stilton or other soft blue cheese into the cooled filling before you put the pastry lids on.

Preparation: 20 minutes
Cooking: 30 minutes
Serves: 4

Frozen Dairy-Free
Christmas Pudding

This delicious alternative to the traditional pudding is irresistible and will appeal to everyone, whilst being dairy-free and gluten-free for those on a special diet.

85 g/3 oz ready-to-eat dried apricots, roughly chopped

85 g/3 oz prunes, roughly chopped

85 g/3 oz seedless raisins

100 ml/3½ fl oz brandy

2 tablespoons custard powder

50 g/2 oz caster sugar

300 ml/½ pint Evernat Hazelnut Drink

250 ml/9 fl oz Provamel Soya Dream

One Place all the fruit in a bowl and pour the brandy over. Cover and leave to stand overnight.

Two Mix the custard powder and sugar with 3 tablespoons of the hazelnut drink. Pour the remainder into a heavy-based saucepan and bring slowly to the boil. Gradually whisk the hot hazelnut drink into the custard powder, then pour the mixture back into the pan. Cook over a low heat, stirring constantly, until thick.

Three Pour the custard into a chilled bowl and leave to cool. Whisk in the Soya Dream and stir in the fruit. Pour the mixture into a shallow freezerproof container and put in the freezer. When the mixture is half frozen, remove from the freezer and whisk to break down the ice crystals, then return to the freezer. Repeat this whisking process once more then spoon the mixture into a 1 litre/1¾ pint pudding basin, cover and freeze until firm.

Four To serve, dip the basin quickly into boiling water, loosen the sides with a palette or blunt-edged knife, then turn out onto a plate.

✱ PREPARING AHEAD: You may freeze the pudding up to 1 month in advance of serving.

Preparation: 30 minutes, plus soaking and freezing time
Cooking: 15 minutes
Serves: 4–6

Iced Raspberry
Cranachan Trifle

This wonderful pudding is loosely based on the Scottish classic, Cranachan, which is a blend of toasted oatmeal, raspberries, whisky and cream.

200 g/8 oz clear honey or golden syrup

175 ml/6 fl oz Scotch whisky

225 g/8 oz fresh or frozen raspberries (thawed if frozen), plus 100 g/4 oz to decorate (optional)

50 g/2 oz oat-based muesli

100 g/4 oz golden caster sugar

500 ml/17 fl oz tub raspberry sorbet

850 ml/1½ pints double cream

8 egg yolks

One Put 4 tablespoons of honey in a small saucepan with 6 tablespoons of whisky and warm gently. Spoon the raspberries into a deep, freezerproof serving bowl and pour the honey mix over them. Lightly stir to mix with the fruit and leave to cool.

Two Put the muesli in a small, thick-bottomed saucepan with the sugar, and gently heat until the sugar forms a clear caramel. Pour on to a lightly oiled baking sheet and leave to cool. When cold, break into rough pieces and put half into the bowl of a food processor or blender and whizz until finely chopped. Store the remainder in an airtight container.

Three When the raspberries are cold, scoop the raspberry sorbet on top of them.

Four Slowly whip 600 ml/1 pint of the double cream, adding the remaining whisky in a steady stream. Be careful not to overwhip – the cream should just hold its shape.

Five Warm the remaining honey in a small saucepan. Put the egg yolks in a bowl and whisk for 4–5 minutes, gradually adding the hot honey until the mixture is pale and lightly thickened. Fold in the whipped cream and blitzed muesli. Spoon this on to the raspberry sorbet and freeze overnight.

Six Whip the remaining double cream, spoon it on top and decorate with the reserved muesli and fresh raspberries, if using. Leave to stand at room temperature for 10 minutes before serving. If you like, serve it with bought or home-made shortbread.

✱ PREPARING AHEAD: You can make the trifle up to the end of step five up to 2 days ahead. Continue from step six just before you are ready to serve it.

Preparation: 1 hour 30 minutes, plus overnight freezing
Serves: 8

BRIAN GLOVER'S

Vanilla and Clementine
Ice Cream Terrine

This is the ultimate freeze-ahead dessert. All you have to do is remove it from the freezer 15–20 minutes before serving so that it is easier to slice.

Preparation: 40 minutes, plus freezing

Cooking: 20 minutes

Serves: 8–10

300 ml/½ pint full-fat milk

1 vanilla pod, split in half
   lengthways

4 egg yolks

100 g/4 oz caster sugar

142 ml/5 fl oz carton double
   cream

200 ml/7 fl oz carton crème
   fraîche

10–12 clementines

250 g/9 oz caster sugar

5–6 cardamom pods,
   lightly crushed

juice of 1 lemon

2 tablespoons Cointreau
   or triple sec

50 g/2 oz amaretti or ratafia
   biscuits, crushed

One Make the vanilla ice cream first. Bring the milk and vanilla pod to the boil, take off the heat and leave to infuse for 30 minutes. Beat together the egg yolks and caster sugar until pale, bring the milk back to the boil, then whisk it into the egg yolks. Pour the mixture into a clean pan and stir constantly without boiling for 5–8 minutes or until the custard coats the back of the spoon. Transfer to a bowl and plunge the base into cold water. Stir frequently until the custard cools.

Two Remove the vanilla pod and scrape the seeds out into the custard, using the tip of a knife. Stir together the double cream and crème fraîche, then stir them into the custard. Churn in an ice cream maker until softly frozen. (If you do not have an ice cream maker, whip the cream until softly stiff then fold into the custard with the crème fraîche. Turn the mixture into a freezer tray and freeze until it is just frozen around the edges. Beat in a food processor or mixer until smooth. Repeat the freezing and beating process twice more.)

Three For the clementine sorbet, take the rind off four of the clementines, leaving no pith. Drop into a saucepan with the sugar, lightly crushed cardamom pods and 250 ml/9 fl oz water. Bring slowly to the boil, stirring to dissolve the sugar, then simmer for 4–5 minutes. Allow to cool, then strain into a bowl. Squeeze the juice from all the clementines into a bowl and add the lemon juice. Strain the citrus juices into the syrup and then stir in the liqueur. Chill, then churn in an ice cream maker until softly frozen. (Otherwise, place in a freezer tray, in a shallow layer, and freeze until slushy then beat as before. Beat the sorbet three times as it freezes.)

Four Pour half the vanilla ice cream mixture into the bottom of a 1 kg /2 lb loaf tin. Level, then return to the freezer for 15 minutes until firm. Spoon all the sorbet over it and level. Return to the freezer for 20 minutes, until firm. Finally spoon the rest of the vanilla ice cream over it and level the surface. Return to the freezer for at least 3 hours, until firm.

Five To turn out the terrine, dip the tin briefly in hot water and then invert onto a serving plate. Allow to soften for 15–20 minutes in the fridge. Just before serving, sprinkle the terrine with the crushed amaretti or ratafia biscuits, then cut into slices.

✱ HAND-MADE ICE CREAM: An ice cream maker will make this an easy pudding to put together but if you haven't got one, then you will need to beat the ice cream several times during freezing.

✱ FREEZING: At the end of step four, cover the terrine, in its tin, with plastic film and leave in the freezer. Do not freeze home-made ices for longer than a couple of weeks as they tend to lose their flavour.

Chocolate
Christmas Pudding

If you prefer a pudding that's light but special enough for Christmas, this is the one for you. It's unashamedly sweet, studded with chunks of chocolate and dates, and the caramel sauce will go down a treat with children. Added to that, it cooks in under 15 minutes in the microwave.

Preparation: 20 minutes	
Cooking: 12–15 minutes, plus 5 minutes resting	
Serves: 8	

100 g/4 oz softened butter

175 g/6 oz dark muscovado sugar

3 eggs

200 g/8 oz self-raising flour

150 ml/¼ pint milk

1 teaspoon ground cinnamon

140 g/5 oz stoned chopped dates

85 g/3 oz dark chocolate, roughly chopped

50 g/2 oz pecan halves

FOR THE SAUCE

175 g/6 oz butter

175 g/6 oz golden syrup

2 tablespoons dark muscovado sugar

single cream, for serving

One Put the butter, sugar, eggs, flour, milk and cinnamon in a bowl and beat with a wooden spoon for 2–3 minutes, or with a hand whisk for 1–2 minutes, until light and fluffy. Stir in the dates, chocolate and pecans. Turn into a buttered 1.2 litre/2 pint basin and cover with plastic film. (You can do this up to 24 hours ahead.)

Two Pierce the plastic film several times (picture 1) and microwave on Medium for 12–15 minutes, until the mixture is firm to the touch and a skewer inserted into the centre comes out clean, apart from traces of melted chocolate. Leave to rest for 5 minutes.

Three Put all the sauce ingredients into a small saucepan and bring to the boil, stirring to melt the butter. Simmer for 1–2 minutes, until syrupy. Turn out the pudding onto a serving plate and pour some of the sauce over it. Serve with cream and the remaining sauce (picture 2).

Stollen

Set aside a couple of pleasant hours to make this stollen, a traditional German sweet festive bread. It's packed with boozy fruit, nuts and almond paste and it is usually served on Christmas Eve with coffee. It'll fill the kitchen with Christmassy aromas and make a light alternative to a traditional cake. It is delicious served for breakfast on Christmas morning.

The raisins, currants, candied peel and almonds are soaked overnight in dark rum and orange and lemon zest. The boozy fruits are then kneaded into a rich buttery dough, which is wrapped around home-made almond paste. Immediately after baking, the bread is finished off with a glaze of butter and a thick dusting of icing sugar. The plump, comforting shape of the bread is said to represent the swaddled baby Jesus in the manger.

Preparation: 20 minutes, plus overnight soaking and 2 hours rising

Cooking: 25–30 minutes

Serves: 14 slices

100 g/4 oz candied lemon

and orange peel

50 g/2 oz blanched almonds

85 g/3 oz raisins

85 g/3 oz currants

6 tablespoons dark rum

finely grated rind of 1 orange

finely grated rind of 1 lemon

450 g/1 lb strong white

bread flour

1 teaspoon salt

2 sachets of fast-action yeast

140 g/5 oz butter

50 g/2 oz golden caster sugar

1 egg

250 ml/9 fl oz hand-hot milk

25 g/1 oz glacé cherries,

quartered

icing sugar, for dusting

FOR THE ALMOND PASTE

50 g/2 oz icing sugar

50 g/2 oz golden caster sugar

100 g/4 oz ground almonds

1 egg yolk

1 tablespoon fresh lemon

juice

One Finely chop the candied lemon and orange peel and roughly chop the almonds (picture 1). Tip the peel and almonds into a bowl with the raisins and currants. Stir in the rum, and orange and lemon rind and mix well (picture 2). Set aside to soak overnight.

Two Tip the flour, salt and yeast into a bowl. Cut 100 g/4 oz butter into chunks and rub into the flour with your fingertips (picture 3). Stir in the sugar. In a separate bowl, beat the egg and mix in the milk. Stir the egg mixture into the flour and mix well to form a dough.

Three Knead the dough on a lightly floured surface for about 10 minutes until smooth and elastic (picture 4). Shape into a ball and put in a clean, lightly greased bowl. Cover with cling film and leave in a warm place for about 1 hour until doubled in size. You will be able to tell whether the dough has risen by lightly pressing the top (picture 5). If the indent your finger makes disappears easily, the dough is ready.

Four To make the almond paste, sift the sugars into a bowl and stir in the ground almonds. Gradually work in the egg yolk and lemon juice with your hands to form a thick paste (picture 6). Knead the paste on a work surface, lightly dusted with icing sugar, until just smooth. Wrap in plastic film and chill until required.

Five Give the risen dough a few punches then knead for 2 minutes. Work in the fruit, nuts and any liquid by gently kneading them into the dough (picture 7). It will take a while, and the mixture will be quite sticky so keep your hands lightly floured. With floured hands, press the dough into a 30 × 20cm/12 × 8in oval.

Six Melt the remaining butter in a small pan (or in the microwave), then brush half the butter over the dough. Scatter the glacé cherry pieces over the dough. Roll the almond paste into a sausage shape slightly shorter than the length of the dough and place along the centre of the dough (picture 8).

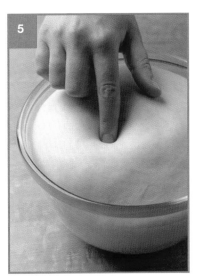

Seven Fold in half, press down lightly and put on a baking sheet (picture 9). Cover loosely with oiled plastic film; leave for 45 minutes–1 hour until it has doubled in size. Preheat oven to 190°C/Gas 5/fan oven 170°C. Bake for 25–30 minutes. Cool for 5 minutes on the sheet. Brush with butter, dust with icing sugar and cool on a wire rack.

✱ STORING THE STOLLEN:
The stollen will keep for 3–4 days wrapped in greaseproof paper and foil, or you can freeze it. Don't dust with icing sugar; wrap the cold loaf in foil and freeze for up to 1 month.

BRIAN GLOVER'S

White Ivy Cake

Brian Glover is one of the most creative cookery writers in Britain, whose recipes are often inspired updates on classic favourites. He is a big fan of Christmas in all its forms.

This cake is for those who like to get more involved with icing their cake and who prefer something a little bit more sophisticated. The ivy leaves are made from ready-to-roll icing using ivy cutters available from a good cookshop; failing that, you can cut some templates out of thin card using a variety of different sized real ivy leaves as a guide. A little edible gold or silver dusting powder, again available from a good cookshop, adds that extra bit of glitz and sparkle.

MAKE THE IVY LEAVES

One Cover the cake with marzipan and ready-to-roll icing or buy one ready iced.

Two Loosely crumple a large sheet of foil and place on a tray. Take half the ready-to-roll icing from a 250g/9oz pack, knead lightly and roll out thinly on a surface dusted with icing sugar.

Three Cut out ivy leaves in two or three different sizes using metal or plastic cutters (or the templates you have cut). Mark the veins with the tip of a knife and place on the crumpled foil to harden so the leaves set in natural curved shapes. Use the remaining paste to make more leaves. You'll need between 50–60 leaves altogether, depending on your design.

ARRANGE THE LEAVES ON THE CAKE

One You can either cover the top of the cake entirely with leaves or shape a simple garland, leaving the centre of the cake exposed, with some of the leaves trailing slightly down the sides.

Two If you have used ready-to-roll icing on your cake, make a thick icing sugar and egg white paste to use as a 'glue' for securing the leaves. If you have Royal-iced the cake yourself, you can simply press the ivy leaves into the icing.

Three Dip a fine paintbrush in silver or gold edible dusting powder and gently flick the powder over the leaves to highlight them. You can also brush the edges of the leaves with the powder to create definition. Twist a length of ribbon and attach to the base of the cake to finish.

Panforte

rice paper, for lining the tin

175 g/6 oz blanched almonds

50 g/2 oz walnut halves

100 g/4 oz shelled hazelnuts

100 g/4 oz dried figs

175 g/6 oz candied citron
 and orange peel

50 g/2 oz plain flour

25 g/1 oz cocoa

1 teaspoon ground cinnamon

½ teaspoon ground
 coriander

¼ teaspoon grated nutmeg

175 g/6 oz granulated sugar

175 g/6 oz clear honey

icing sugar, for dusting

This traditional Italian Christmas cake from Sienna makes a gorgeous gift. When wrapped in plastic film it will keep for up to 2 months. Serve cut into very thin wedges after a meal or at teatime instead of traditional cake. Mixing the honey into the dry ingredients can be hard work, but persevere until all the dry ingredients look moist.

Preparation: 45-50 minutes
Cooking: 45 minutes
Serves: 20–24 wedges

One Preheat the oven to 180°C/Gas 4/fan oven 160°C. Lightly oil a 20 cm/8 in sandwich tin and line the base and sides with rice paper, cutting it to fit (picture 1).

Two In a dry frying pan, toast the nuts until lightly tinged. Roughly chop the nuts, finely chop the figs and peel (picture 2), and mix together. Sift in the flour, cocoa and spices and mix together.

Three Heat the sugar and honey gently in a pan, stirring until the sugar has dissolved. Increase the heat and boil for 2 minutes, until slightly syrupy. Stir into the dry mix (picture 3).

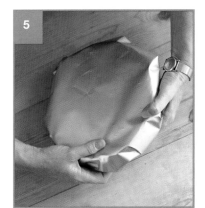

Four Spoon the mixture into the tin and press down (picture 4). Bake for 45 minutes, then cool for 15 minutes. Turn out and cool on a wire rack. Sift icing sugar over the top and wrap in plastic film.

✱ PREPARING AHEAD: You can make the panforte any time from early November as it keeps for up to 2 months. Wrap first in plastic film and then in foil.

✱ HOW TO GIFT WRAP IN STYLE: Wrap the Panforte in plastic film and then in matt silver paper (picture 5) – it is better than shiny as the creases don't show so much. Run gold elasticated string around the package (picture 6). Finish it off with blobs of red sealing wax and stamp with a seal if you have one (picture 7), or leave as red shiny blobs.

Boxing Day
Soup

This warming and comforting meal is a creative way to use leftover vegetables. Meat-eaters can use turkey stock if they have it.

1 tablespoon sunflower oil

1 medium onion, chopped

2 celery sticks, chopped

2 medium potatoes, about 350 g/12 oz total weight, peeled and cut into small chunks

1 tablespoon curry paste

1.2 litres/2 pints vegetable stock, made from stock cubes or granules

550 g/1 lb 4 oz leftover roasted or boiled vegetables, such as Brussels sprouts, carrots, parsnips and squash, roughly chopped

hot water or vegetable stock, as required

natural yogurt or crème fraîche, to serve

Preparation: 10 minutes
Cooking: 30 minutes
Serves: 4

One Heat the oil in a large saucepan and fry the onion for 5 minutes until golden. Stir in the celery and fry for 5 minutes, then tip in the potatoes and fry for a further 1–2 minutes, stirring often.

Two Stir in the curry paste, let it cook for a minute or so, then pour in the stock. Bring to the boil and stir well. Lower the heat, cover and simmer for 15–20 minutes until the potatoes are tender.

Three Tip the leftover vegetables into the pan and warm through for a few minutes. Pour the soup into a food processor or blender and blitz to a smooth purée. Thin down to the consistency you like with hot water or stock (we added 300 ml/$\frac{1}{2}$ pint), then taste for seasoning. Cool and freeze (for up to 1 month), or serve in bowls with spoonfuls of yogurt or crème fraîche swirled on top.

Sherried Turkey and Ham Bake

An all-in-one sauce makes this dish so simple. It's ideal for lunch or supper and a great way of using up leftover turkey.

350 g/12 oz cooked turkey, cut into strips

140 g/5 oz thickly sliced cooked ham, cut into strips

175 g/6 oz frozen peas

50 g/2 oz butter, plus a little extra for greasing the dish

50 g/2 oz plain flour

600 ml/1 pint milk

3 tablespoons medium sherry

2 teaspoons wholegrain mustard

100 g/4 oz Cheddar cheese, grated

50 g/2 oz chopped mixed nuts, such as hazelnuts, almonds and walnuts

One Preheat the oven to 200°C/Gas 6/fan oven 180°C. Mix the turkey, ham and frozen peas together in a buttered ovenproof dish.

Two To make the sauce, put the butter, flour and milk in a saucepan and bring to the boil, whisking all the time, until the sauce is thickened and smooth. Stir in the sherry and mustard, season to taste and simmer for 1 minute. Remove from the heat and stir in half the cheese.

Three To finish, pour the sauce over the ingredients in the dish. Mix the remaining cheese with the nuts and sprinkle on top. Bake for 25–35 minutes until the topping is golden and the sauce is bubbling.

✱ PREPARING AHEAD: Once you've assembled the pie and before baking, you can keep it in the fridge for up to 5 hours or freeze it. (Defrost in fridge overnight, or in the microwave before baking.)

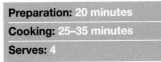

Preparation: 20 minutes
Cooking: 25–35 minutes
Serves: 4

Winter
Crunch Salad

Vary the salad ingredients according to what you've got in the fridge. You can use any leftover cheese instead of Stilton.

1 × 170 g ready-to-bake garlic bread

2 heads chicory

2 celery sticks, cut into thin diagonal slices

1 bunch of radishes, trimmed and quartered

50 g/2 oz shelled walnuts or pecans, toasted and roughly chopped

2 red-skinned eating apples, cored and cut into slim wedges

175 g/6 oz Stilton

4–5 tablespoons ready-made honey and mustard dressing, to serve

One Preheat the oven and cook the garlic bread according to the packet's instructions.

Two Separate the chicory into leaves and toss in a large bowl with the celery, radishes, nuts and apples. Crumble the Stilton in large chunks over the top.

Three Cut half the garlic bread into the marked slices. Cut the remainder into chunks and toss into the salad with as much dressing as you like. Serve with the slices of garlic bread on the side.

Preparation: 15 minutes
Cooking: 10 minutes
Serves: 4

SILVANA FRANCO'S

Christmas Pudding
Ice Cream

This is the easiest ice cream recipe ever. It is so good we recommend you save some of the pudding from Christmas dinner to make it.

200 g/8 oz cold leftover Christmas pudding

4 tablespoons dark rum or brandy

1 litre/1¾ pint tub vanilla ice cream

One Crumble the Christmas pudding into a bowl and drizzle over the rum or brandy. Set aside for 1 hour or so until all the liquid has been absorbed.

Two Remove the ice cream from the freezer and put in the fridge for 30 minutes to soften slightly. Empty the ice cream into a bowl and beat with a wooden spoon until smooth. Stir in the pudding, then spoon the mixture into a rigid plastic container and refreeze until solid.

Three Remove from the freezer 20 minutes before serving. It's delicious served in scoops on its own or drizzled with extra cream.

**Preparation: 5 minutes,
plus 1 hour soaking**

Serves: 6–8

More ways with leftover Christmas pudding

BRANDY-BUTTERED CHRISTMAS PUDDING

Melt a knob of brandy butter in a frying pan and fry 2 slices of Christmas pudding until hot. Serve with single cream.

CHRISTMAS PUDDING CHOCOLATE CAKE

Crumble 300 g/10 oz Christmas pud into 100 g/4 oz melted chocolate and mix. Stir in 6 crushed digestive biscuits. Spoon into a 20 cm/8 in round cake tin lined with plastic film. Chill until firm, then cut into wedges.

BAKED CHRISTMAS PUDDING

Cut one thick slice of pud per person and put in a shallow ovenproof dish. Dot with butter, sprinkle with demerara sugar, cover with foil and bake at 180°C/Gas 4/fan oven 160°C for 20–25 minutes until piping hot.

Mix it!

Sarah Jane Evans, Associate Editor on *Good Food Magazine*, gets adventurous with mixed drinks to enjoy over the holiday season.

Cocktails

MARGARITA

The key ingredient of margarita is tequila, the national spirit of Mexico. Tequila is made from the fermented juice of the agave, the local cactus. A margarita, with its sudden hit of salt and citrus, is a welcome palate-cleanser in the midst of Christmas excess.

Shake equal measures of tequila and Cointreau with the juice of half a lime and lots of ice. Dip a finger into the liquid and run it round the rim of a glass. Up-end the glass in a saucer of coarse sea salt. Strain the drink into the glass.

Serves 1

COCONUT TEQUILA

While you still have some tequila left in the bottle, try this creamy recipe.

Put a measure of tequila in a blender with 2 teaspoons each lemon juice and coconut cream, and crushed ice. Blend and strain into a glass to serve.

Serves 1

PINK GIN

For authenticity this 1940s favourite should be made with Plymouth gin, which you can now buy once more. (angostura bitters, which make the gin pink, are an excellent digestif. Add a few drops to ice cold soda or tonic.)

Shake several drops of angostura bitters into a glass, roll round the glass, then pour away. Add a measure of Plymouth gin; ice is optional.

Serves 1

GIMLET

While you've got the bottle handy, stir a measure of Plymouth gin and half a measure of Rose's Lime Cordial in a glass with ice and serve. Very refreshing, and a nice change from the classic gin, tonic and lemon.

Serves 1

DRY MARTINI

People have written books (or at least chapters) about this one. James Bond got it all wrong – shaking is not correct. The point is the vermouth – or lack of it.

Pour a dash (only) of dry white vermouth (Martini or another make) into a measuring jug, swirl and pour away. Add 4 measures of ice-cold gin and ice, then strain into cocktail glasses. Squeeze lemon peel to release drops of lemon oil into the glass, or add a green cocktail olive.

Serves 4

BLOODY MARY

The star refresher the day after a big party. Be sure you have all the ingredients if you are having friends over on 1 January.

Put 2 or 3 ice cubes in a tall glass. Add a slice of lemon, 1 teaspoon Worcestershire sauce, 1/2 teaspoon lemon juice, 2–3 drops of Tabasco sauce, a pinch of celery salt, several good grindings of black pepper and a pinch of salt. Top up the glass to 3/4 full with tomato juice. Add in a measure of vodka (or more to taste) and stir. Garnish with a celery stick. Some people like to add a little dry sherry.

Serves 1

OLD FASHIONED

In a tumbler, grind a sugar lump with 1–2 shakes of angostura bitters and a measure of American rye whiskey. Add a slice of lemon and a stirrer, then a slice of orange and a cocktail cherry, if liked.

Serves 1

WHISKY MCVITAL

Michael van Straten's book Super Juice (Mitchell Beazley) makes a great gift for those who want to start the new year full of vitality. This spin on a hot toddy is rich in bioflavonoids and vitamin C so it is great for warding off colds, while the gingerols from the ginger are good for coughs.

In a juicer, process 2 peeled oranges (leave the pith behind), 1 peeled lime, 1 peeled lemon, 175 g/6 oz white seedless grapes and 15g/1/2 oz fresh root ginger. Stir 2 shots of whisky into the juice. If you like, top up with boiling water to make a hot toddy.

Serves 1–2

Warming drinks

MULLED WINE

Two things to remember with mulled wine – always use good quality wine, as mulling does not disguise plonk; and don't let it boil or you will drive off the alcohol and be left with a drink lacking any kick.

To each bottle of red wine add 150 ml/1/4 pint ruby port, and 75 ml/21/2 fl oz each of cognac and Cointreau or Grand Marnier. Add 1–2 tablespoons light muscovado sugar to taste, 2 cinnamon sticks, a whole nutmeg, and as many clove-studded orange and lemon slices as there are guests. Stir continuously to dissolve the sugar, then keep on a low simmer for 10 minutes. Serve in warmed heatproof glasses.

Serves 6–8

POLISH MULLED VODKA

This is a much more alcoholic version of a mull. Ideal for warming up on New Year's Eve, if you're attending an outdoor celebration.

Heat 6 tablespoons clear honey in a large pan with 300 ml/1/2 pint water. When the honey has dissolved, stir in a vanilla pod, a cinnamon stick, 6 cloves, and the rind of an orange and a melon cut into thin strips. Cover and simmer for 5 minutes. Remove from the heat and leave to stand for an hour or more. Strain into a pan, add a bottle of vodka, warm through and serve in warmed heatproof glasses.

Serves 12

Low/No Alcohol

FRESH FIZZ

Cranberry juice is a great base for long non-alcoholic drinks as it's not too sweet.

Dilute cranberry juice with fizzy water or lemon/limeade. Or, for a variation on a spritzer, top up a cranberry juice with sparkling wine.

SOFT OPTIONS

Have plenty of sparkling water, plus good quality fruit squashes and cordials such as Rock's Organic Fruit Squashes or Belvoir Fruit Cordials (both widely available), which can be diluted to taste. Another must-have at this time of year is traditional ginger beer. The heat of the ginger drives out the cold, and the spice aids the digestion when there are plenty of rich foods about.

Glögg

This warm spiced wine is traditionally served in small cups with a teaspoon, so you can eat the alcohol-soaked almonds and raisins as you drink the wine.

10 cardamom pods,
  split in half
2 cinnamon sticks
6 cloves
100 g/4 oz piece of fresh
  root ginger, sliced
1 bottle red wine
85 g/3 oz caster sugar
a shot of vodka
flaked almonds and raisins,
  to serve

One Put the spices in a saucepan with the wine and sugar. Bring to the boil.

Two Simmer very gently for 5 minutes, then turn off the heat. Cover and leave to infuse for 15 minutes.

Three Add the vodka. Serve with a few flaked almonds and raisins in each glass.

Preparation: 5 minutes
Cooking: 5 minutes, plus 15 minutes infusing
Serves: 10

Index

For my husband, Mick

ACKNOWLEDGEMENTS

Many thanks to all the wonderful *Good*
Food **team, especially Orlando Murrin,**
Angela Nilsen, Vicky Musselman and Lynne
Stanford who gave me such great support
during the planning, testing, writing and
photographing of this book. I would also
particularly like to thank Jeni Wright who
supplied the Roast Goose recipe, Fiona
Hunter for the Frozen Christmas Pudding,
Moyra Fraser for the recipes on pages 98
and 120, and Joanna Farrow who supplied
the recipes on pages 16, 17, 28, 42, 54, 55,
66 and 68.

MARY CADOGAN is a highly respected
food writer with a wealth of experience
in many areas of the food world. Before
joining *BBC Good Food Magazine*, Mary
contributed regularly to several national
magazines and was a top food stylist
specializing in food photography. She is
also the author of several best-selling
cookery books. Mary was appointed
Deputy Editor of *Good Food* in 1993 and
became Food Director in 2000. During
her time there, in addition to writing her
popular food features in the magazine,
she has been responsible for ensuring
that all the recipes taste great, work
perfectly and are beautifully photographed.

Published by BBC Worldwide Ltd,
Woodlands, 80 Wood Lane,
London W12 OTT

First published in paperback in 1999.
This hardback edition, with extra recipes, published in 2002.

This compilation copyright © BBC Worldwide 2002
Celebrity recipes copyright © individual contributors 1999
The moral right of the authors has been asserted

Principal photographer: Marie-Louise Avery

Additional photography:
Chocolate Chestnut Log (page 26), Brian Glover's Vanilla and
    Clementine Ice Cream Terrine (page 122): Linda Burgess
Canapés without Tears (pages 60–5): Philip Webb
Christmas on a Special Diet (pages 94–5): William Reavell
Edible Gifts (pages 16, 17, 28, 54, 55, 66, 68), Frozen Dairy-Free
    Christmas Pudding (page 118): Simon Smith
Glazed Ham with Caramelized Fruits (page 42), Roast Goose
    (page 104), Manju Malhi's Masala Nut Roast (page 114):
    Martin Thompson
Platter of Arbroath Smokies (page 98), Potted Ham with Beetroot and
    Red Onion Salad (page 100), Mixed Mushroom and Chestnut Pies
    (page 116), Iced Raspberry Cranachan Trifle (page 120), Boxing Day
    Soup (page 134), Sherried Turkey and Ham Bake (page 135),
    Winter Crunch Salad (page 136): Roger Stowell
Silvana Franco's Christmas Pudding Ice Cream (page 138): Ian Wallace
Celeriac and Parsley Soup with Crumbled Stilton (page 102),
    Beef Wellington (page 110): Ken Field
Glazed Turkey Crown (page 108), Chocolate Christmas Pudding
    (page 124), Panforte (page 132): Geoff Wilkinson
Salmon and Watercress Puff (page 112): Jean Cazals
Stollen (page 126), Brian Glover's White Ivy Cake (page 130):
    David Munns
(all photographs © BBC Worldwide, 1999 and 2002)

All the recipes in this book have been previously published in
BBC Good Food Magazine

ISBN 0 563 48850 6

Project Editors: Rachel Brown and April Warman
Copy editors: Christine King and Melanie Leyshon
Designers: John Calvert, Isobel Gillan and Rachel Hardman Carter
Cover designer: Jason Vrakas
Production Controllers: Susan Currie and Christopher Tinker

Set in Helvetica
Printed and bound in France by Imprimerie Pollina s.a. : L87313
Colour separations by Radstock Reproductions, Midsomer Norton,
    Somerset

Back cover photographs
TOP: *Canapés* (pages 60–5)
CENTRE: *Turkey and all the Trimmings* (pages 82–91)
BOTTOM: *Festive Mince Pies* (pages 20–1)